Mediterranea Blue Zones Diet Cookbook

The Simple & Easy Longevity Diet Recipes Cooking Book for Beginners (Sardinia, Italy and Ikaria, Greece)

Blue Zone Eating Book 2

Dr. Allison Parker

Table of Contents

Chapter 1: 7

Introduction to Mediterranean Blue Zones Diet.................7

Chapter 2: 9

The Blue Zones of Sardinia, Italy, and Ikaria, Greece: Insights into Longevity..9

Chapter 3: 13

Essential Ingredients of the Mediterranean Blue Zones Diet 13

3.1 Olive Oil: The Liquid Gold.....................................13

3.2 Fresh Vegetables and Greens: A Vault of Vitamins..16

3.3 Legumes and Pulses: The Protein Powerhouses.......19

3.4 Whole Grains: Sustaining Energy and Vitality.........22

Chapter 4: 27

Cooking Techniques of the Mediterranean Blue Zones......27

4.1 Grilling and Roasting: Enhancing Flavor with Minimal Ingredients 27

4.2 Simmering and Braising: Slow-Cooked Comfort Foods 30

4.3 Marinating and Pickling: Preserving Freshness and Flavor...33

Chapter 5: 37

Breakfasts in the Blue Zones: Energizing Morning Meals..37

5.1 Greek Yogurt Parfait with Honey and Walnuts 37

5.2 Sardinian Frittata with Fresh Herbs and Tomatoes .40

5.3 Ikarian Oatmeal with Dates and Almonds 42
5.4 Sardinian Pane Carasau with Ricotta and Honey 45
5.5 Ikarian Herbal Tea and Fig Bars 47
5.6 Sardinian Pecorino and Pear Omelette 50
5.7 Ikarian Honeyed Yogurt with Pistachios 52
5.8 Sardinian Tomato and Basil Bruschetta.................. 55
5.9 Ikarian Wild Green Pie (Hortopita) 59
5.10 Sardinian Artichoke and Mint Frittata 62
Chapter 6: 67
Mediterranean Lunches: Wholesome Midday Meals 67
6.1 Greek Salad with Feta Cheese and Kalamata Olives 67
6.2 Sardinian Minestrone Soup with Cannellini Beans and Kale 70
6.3 Ikarian Lentil Stew with Vegetables and Herbs........ 73
6.4 Sardinian Pecorino and Fig Salad 75
6.5 Ikarian Fisherman's Soup... 78
6.6 Sardinian Pasta with Bottarga 81
6.7 Ikarian Chickpea and Spinach Salad 85
6.8 Sardinian Roasted Lamb with Rosemary and Garlic 88
6.9 Ikarian Wild Herb Pie... 91
6.10 Sardinian Fava Bean and Pecorino Cheese Dip 95
Chapter 7: 99
Dinners from the Blue Zones: Flavorful Evening Dishes ... 99
7.1 Grilled Fish with Lemon and Garlic from Ikaria....... 99

7.2 Sardinian Seafood Pasta with Cherry Tomatoes and Basil....103

7.3 Greek Moussaka with Eggplant and Bechamel Sauce 106

7.4 Sardinian Roasted Pork with Myrtle....110

7.5 Ikarian Longevity Stew....112

7.6 Sardinian Clam and Fennel Soup....115

7.7 Grilled Octopus over Ikarian Fava....118

7.8 Sardinian Culurgiones....121

7.9 Ikarian Baked Sardines....125

7.10 Sardinian Lamb with Artichokes....128

Chapter 8:....133

Snacks and Sweets Inspired by the Mediterranean Blue Zones....133

8.1 Ikarian Hummus with Roasted Red Pepper and Chickpeas....133

8.2 Sardinian Olive Oil Cake with Orange Zest and Almonds....137

8.3 Greek Baklava with Honey and Pistachios....140

8.4 Sardinian Pistachio Biscotti....143

8.5 Ikarian Fig and Walnut Tart....146

8.6 Sardinian Honey and Almond Nougat (Torrone)....149

8.7 Ikarian Petimezi Cookies....152

8.8 Sardinian Seadas....155

8.9 Ikarian Herbal Tea Infusion....158

8.10 Sardinian Ricotta and Lemon Cake....161

Chapter 9: 165

Lifestyle Tips for Longevity: Beyond Diet 165

9.1 Enjoying Meals with Family and Friends: The Importance of Social Connections 166

9.2 Physical Activity in the Blue Zones: Embracing an Active Lifestyle 168

9.3 Stress Reduction and Mindfulness: Cultivating Inner Peace 171

Conclusion: 175

Embracing the Mediterranean Blue Zones Diet for Health and Longevity 175

Glossary of Mediterranean Ingredients and Terms 179

30-Day Mediterranean Blue Zones Diet Meal Plan 183

Acknowledgments 193

Chapter 1:

Introduction to Mediterranean Blue Zones Diet

Welcome to the sun-drenched shores of the Mediterranean, where the sea sparkles under an endless sky and the land is lush with bountiful vineyards, olive groves, and gardens bursting with fresh produce. In this chapter, we explore the Mediterranean diet, not just as a mere eating plan but as a celebration of vibrant flavors and a testament to a lifestyle that has captivated health experts and enthusiasts around the globe.

The Mediterranean diet is renowned for its correlation with prolonged life expectancy and significantly lower rates of chronic diseases. The essence of this diet is deeply rooted in the eating habits of the populations living in the Blue Zones of Sardinia, Italy, and Ikaria, Greece—regions celebrated for their unusually high number of centenarians and profound health statistics.

What exactly makes the Mediterranean diet so beneficial? It is characterized by a generous use of olive oil, an abundance of fresh vegetables and fruits, the consumption of whole grains, and a preference for lean proteins like fish and legumes over red meat.

Herbs and spices replace salt, and meals are often accompanied by a glass of red wine, enjoyed in moderation. But beyond the food, it is the Mediterranean approach to eating—savoring each meal slowly and in the company of others—that contributes significantly to overall well-being.

In Sardinia and Ikaria, meals are more than just sustenance; they are social and familial gatherings, opportunities to connect with others and celebrate life. This social aspect, combined with physical activity from daily walks and gardening, forms a holistic approach to health that extends beyond the dinner table.

As we delve into the Mediterranean Blue Zones Diet, we'll uncover the secrets behind the longevity of its people and learn how to incorporate their age-old wisdom into our modern lives. Whether you're looking to revitalize your eating habits or simply curious about this acclaimed diet, the journey through these enchanting Mediterranean lands will offer insights and inspiration to nourish both body and soul. Let's embark on this culinary voyage together, exploring the simple yet profound practices that make the Mediterranean diet a true blueprint for a long and healthy life.

Chapter 2:

The Blue Zones of Sardinia, Italy, and Ikaria, Greece: Insights into Longevity

In the quest to uncover the secrets of longevity, few places offer more compelling evidence than the Mediterranean Blue Zones of Sardinia, Italy, and Ikaria, Greece. These regions are not only known for their idyllic landscapes and rich history, but also for their remarkable concentrations of centenarians—people who live to or beyond the age of 100. What is it about these places that cultivates such extraordinary longevity? This chapter delves into the lifestyles and eating habits that define these areas and how they contribute to the health and longevity of their populations.

Sardinia, Italy

Located in the Mediterranean Sea, Sardinia boasts a rugged landscape, with mountainous terrains that naturally encourage physical activity such as herding and farming. The traditional Sardinian diet is a perfect illustration of the Mediterranean diet, characterized by its high consumption of legumes, whole grains, vegetables, and fruits, along with a moderate intake of dairy products from sheep and goats. Central to their diet is also the consumption of lean proteins from sources like fish and poultry, with red meat consumed only occasionally.

One of the staples of the Sardinian diet is the local bread, pane carasau, which can be kept for days without losing its freshness. Sardinians also consume a considerable amount of pecorino cheese—made from sheep's milk—which is high in omega-3 fatty acids due to the animals grazing on omega-3 rich grasses. Perhaps most notably, Sardinians regularly drink Cannonau wine, which has two to three times the level of artery-scrubbing flavonoids as other wines.

Social structure plays a crucial role as well. Sardinians maintain strong family ties and a sense of community that provides both emotional and logistical support. Meals are often communal, a practice that reinforces social bonds and leads to psychological well-being, which is a vital component of longevity.

Ikaria, Greece

Ikaria, an island in the Aegean Sea, is another renowned Blue Zone, where the population is known for its significant number of elderly citizens, low rates of chronic disease, and minimal stress levels. Ikarians live by a diet that emphasizes vegetables, fruits, whole grains, beans, potatoes, and olive oil. Meat is eaten sparingly, reserved mainly for festivals or as an accompaniment, not the centerpiece of meals.

A signature aspect of the Ikarian diet is the liberal use of herbal teas. Locals frequently consume teas made from wild herbs like rosemary, sage, and oregano, which are thought to have anti-inflammatory and antioxidant properties. Ikarians also partake in a moderate daily intake of coffee and wine, which are believed to contribute to their overall cardiovascular health.

The pace of life in Ikaria is slow, fostering low stress levels and a daily routine that includes regular naps and community interaction. Physical activity is seamlessly integrated into their daily lives, with most Ikarians engaged in gardening, walking, and fishing.

Lessons from the Blue Zones

Both Sardinian and Ikarian lifestyles highlight critical aspects that contribute to longevity: a diet rich in plant-based foods and lean proteins, moderate physical activity, strong social connections, and a balanced approach to life that includes stress management. These regions demonstrate that longevity is not just about diet but is also deeply influenced by lifestyle and cultural practices.

In exploring these Blue Zones, we are reminded that the secret to a long life does not lie in a single ingredient or diet but in a holistic approach to living. The Mediterranean Blue Zones offer invaluable lessons on how integrating healthful eating habits with a supportive social structure and an active lifestyle can lead to a fuller, more rewarding life.

Chapter 3:

Essential Ingredients of the Mediterranean Blue Zones Diet

In the Mediterranean Blue Zones, longevity is not just a hope but a realistic outcome, supported by a diet rich in life-sustaining nutrients and ingredients that are as simple as they are ancient. The secret to the remarkable health and longevity enjoyed by the residents of Sardinia, Italy, and Ikaria, Greece, lies in their daily consumption of certain key ingredients. These staples are not only fundamental to their culinary practices but are deeply embedded within their cultural heritage, making their diet a profound expression of their way of life.

This chapter dives into the core components of the Mediterranean Blue Zones diet, revealing how each ingredient contributes to health and longevity. These ingredients are readily available, affordable, and versatile, making it easy for anyone, anywhere, to incorporate them into their daily meals.

3.1 Olive Oil: The Liquid Gold

Olive oil, especially extra virgin olive oil, is revered not just as a food but as a cultural icon in Mediterranean cuisine. Its ubiquitous use in cooking, as a finisher, and even as a base for dressings, speaks to its vital role in the diets of those living in the Blue Zones of the Mediterranean. Extracted through the cold-pressing of olives, extra virgin olive oil retains the pure essence of the fruit, including its rich flavor and health-enhancing properties.

Nutritional Profile

Extra virgin olive oil is high in monounsaturated fats, primarily oleic acid, which is known for its ability to affect cholesterol levels positively. This type of fat is much more stable under heat, making olive oil a safe choice for cooking compared to other oils which may release harmful compounds when heated. Beyond fats, it is also a valuable source of tocopherols (vitamin E) and polyphenols, which provide potent antioxidant effects.

Health Benefits

The health benefits of olive oil are extensive and supported by numerous studies:

- **Heart Health**: Regular consumption of olive oil has been shown to lower the levels of total cholesterol and LDL-cholesterol ("bad" cholesterol) in the blood. It can also improve the lining of blood vessels and may help prevent excessive blood clotting, thus reducing the risk of stroke and heart attack.

- **Anti-inflammatory Properties**: The phenolic compounds in olive oil, including oleocanthal, have anti-inflammatory properties comparable to ibuprofen. This makes it effective in reducing the systemic inflammation that can lead to various chronic diseases.
- **Cancer Prevention**: Antioxidants in olive oil can help protect the body from cellular damage that can lead to a range of cancers. Studies suggest a link between the consistent intake of olive oil and reduced risks of breast and colorectal cancers.
- **Digestive Health**: Olive oil aids in the digestive process by stimulating the gallbladder to release bile, an important substance needed to digest fats.

Culinary Uses

In the kitchen, olive oil is as versatile as it is healthful. It can be used for sautéing vegetables, grilling fish or meat, and creating robust sauces. As a dressing, it pairs beautifully with both vinegar and lemon juice, enhancing salads with its smooth, fruity profile. It's also perfect for drizzling over cooked dishes, where its raw flavor can be fully appreciated.

Cultural Significance

In Mediterranean culture, olive oil is more than just an ingredient; it's a symbol of life and vitality. It has historical significance in religious and spiritual rituals, and continues to be a staple in daily life, consumed with almost every meal. This longstanding tradition of olive oil consumption is a testament to its enduring appeal and testament to its health benefits.

Embracing olive oil in your daily diet can be a simple step toward a healthier lifestyle, reflecting the longevity practices of the Mediterranean's Blue Zones. Whether integrating it into cooking or enjoying it in its raw form, olive oil is truly a liquid gold, offering a blend of flavor and health benefits that few other ingredients can match.

3.2 Fresh Vegetables and Greens: A Vault of Vitamins

The Mediterranean diet's emphasis on fresh vegetables and greens is not only a feast for the eyes but also a foundation for good health. The array of colors found in Mediterranean dishes is a direct reflection of the variety of nutrients these vegetables provide. Each hue represents different antioxidants and phytonutrients, which play crucial roles in maintaining physical health and preventing disease.

Nutritional Richness

Leafy greens such as spinach, kale, and Swiss chard are celebrated for their high levels of vitamins A, C, K, and several B vitamins. These nutrients are essential for maintaining good vision, immune function, blood clotting, and energy production. Additionally, they are excellent sources of dietary fiber, which promotes digestive health by helping to maintain regular bowel movements and by feeding the beneficial bacteria in the gut.

Cruciferous vegetables like broccoli, cabbage, and Brussels sprouts are rich in glucosinolates, compounds that have been studied for their cancer-protective properties. When consumed, these compounds are broken down into biologically active compounds that have been shown to inhibit the growth of cancer cells in animal and test-tube studies.

Health Benefits

The benefits of consuming a wide variety of vegetables include:

- **Reduced Inflammation**: Many vegetables in the Mediterranean diet, especially leafy greens, contain anti-inflammatory compounds that can reduce the risk of chronic diseases associated with inflammation, such as heart disease, diabetes, and arthritis.
- **Antioxidant Protection**: Antioxidants in vegetables help neutralize harmful free radicals in the body. This protection can lessen the oxidative stress that contributes to aging and many chronic conditions.

- **Support Weight Management**: Vegetables have a high water and fiber content, making them low in calories but high in volume. They can help you feel full longer without adding excess calories, which is beneficial for weight control.

Culinary Uses

In Mediterranean cuisine, vegetables are not just side dishes but are often the star of the meal. They can be enjoyed in a multitude of ways:

- **Raw**: Fresh in salads or as part of an antipasto platter.
- **Cooked**: Grilled, roasted, or sautéed with a splash of olive oil and a pinch of salt.
- **Blended**: Into soups and sauces, where they add flavor and thickness without heavy creams or flours.
- **Stuffed**: Bell peppers, zucchini, and tomatoes filled with a mixture of grains, herbs, and spices, then baked.

Cultural Significance

In the Mediterranean, the daily consumption of fresh vegetables and greens is more than just a dietary habit; it's a way of life that celebrates the seasons, local produce, and communal eating. Meals are designed around what is available and fresh, ensuring that dishes are both nutritious and delicious. This connection to the land and its bounty is a fundamental aspect of the culture and is intrinsic to the region's health and longevity.

Incorporating a variety of fresh vegetables and greens into your diet can significantly impact your health and well-being, mirroring the dietary practices of the Mediterranean's Blue Zones. These ingredients offer a delicious and natural way to boost nutritional intake and support a long and healthy life.

3.3 Legumes and Pulses: The Protein Powerhouses

Legumes and pulses are vital components of the Mediterranean diet and are highly valued for their nutritional benefits and versatility in cooking. As primary sources of plant-based protein, beans, lentils, chickpeas, and other legumes play a crucial role in the dietary patterns of the Mediterranean Blue Zones, where meat is often consumed sparingly.

Nutritional Benefits

Legumes are not only rich in protein, which is essential for muscle repair and growth, but they are also excellent sources of complex carbohydrates, fiber, iron, folate, magnesium, potassium, and B vitamins. Their high fiber content is particularly beneficial, aiding in digestion and promoting a feeling of fullness, which can help in weight management. Fiber also plays a significant role in regulating blood sugar levels, making legumes ideal for individuals with diabetes or those looking to stabilize their energy throughout the day.

Cardiovascular Health

One of the standout benefits of legumes is their impact on heart health. The soluble fiber found in these foods helps lower cholesterol levels, reducing the risk of heart disease. Moreover, legumes contain significant amounts of antioxidants and anti-inflammatory properties, which protect against the buildup of plaque in the arteries, further promoting cardiovascular health.

Sustainability and Affordability

Legumes are not only good for our bodies but also for the planet. They have a low environmental footprint as they require relatively little water compared to other protein sources like meat and dairy. They also enrich the soil by fixing nitrogen, reducing the need for chemical fertilizers. Economically, legumes are cost-effective, making them accessible to a wide range of people, which is particularly important in the economically diverse regions of the Mediterranean.

Culinary Versatility

The culinary uses of legumes in Mediterranean cuisine are vast and varied:

- **Soups and Stews**: From the classic Italian minestrone to the hearty Greek fasolada, legumes are often the backbone of nourishing soups and stews.
- **Salads**: Chickpeas, lentils, and white beans make excellent additions to salads, providing protein, texture, and flavor.
- **Dips and Spreads**: Hummus, made from chickpeas, is a popular dip throughout the Mediterranean and Middle East and is often served with olive oil and pita bread.
- **Main Dishes**: Legumes are frequently used in place of meat in many traditional dishes, such as falafel made from ground chickpeas or lentil-based meatballs.

Cultural Significance

In the Mediterranean, legumes have been a dietary staple for centuries, often associated with longevity and good health. Their ability to be stored dry for extended periods has historically made them an essential food during times when fresh produce was not available. Today, they continue to be celebrated in traditional feasts and everyday meals, embodying the simplicity and healthfulness of Mediterranean cuisine.

Embracing legumes and pulses in your diet can lead to significant health benefits. Incorporating these protein powerhouses into daily meals can help mimic the dietary habits of the longest-living populations in the Mediterranean, contributing to a healthier and potentially longer life.

3.4 Whole Grains: Sustaining Energy and Vitality

In the heart of the Mediterranean diet lies a profound respect for whole grains, which are integral to nearly every meal in regions like Sardinia and Ikaria. Whole grains such as barley, whole wheat, and oats are cherished not only for their robust flavors and textures but also for their substantial health benefits and the sustained energy they provide.

Nutritional Profile of Whole Grains

Whole grains are the entire seed of a plant and include all three key parts: the bran, germ, and endosperm. This is in contrast to refined grains, which retain only the endosperm after processing. Because whole grains include the bran and germ, they provide a wealth of nutrients that are often lost during refining. These include:

- **Fiber**: Essential for healthy digestion, and helps to prevent constipation. Soluble fiber, found in oats and barley, is particularly beneficial for controlling blood sugar and lowering cholesterol.

- **Proteins**: Important for muscle repair and growth.
- **B Vitamins**: Vital for various metabolic processes.
- **Antioxidants**: Such as phytic acid, ferulic acid, and sulfides, which protect the body against disease.
- **Minerals**: Including iron, magnesium, and zinc, which play crucial roles in numerous bodily functions.

Health Benefits

The inclusion of whole grains in a diet has been linked to numerous health benefits:

- **Reduced Risk of Chronic Diseases**: Regular consumption of whole grains has been shown to reduce the risk of heart disease, stroke, cancer, and diabetes. Studies have consistently demonstrated that whole grain intake is associated with lower levels of cholesterol and triglycerides in the blood.
- **Weight Management**: The fiber in whole grains helps to regulate the body's use of sugars, keeping hunger and blood sugar in check, which can aid in weight management.
- **Digestive Health**: Fiber from whole grains helps provide bulk to stools and promotes healthy gut

bacteria, reducing the risk of inflammation-related conditions such as diverticulitis.

Culinary Uses

Whole grains are remarkably versatile in cooking and can be incorporated into the diet in various ways:

- **Breakfast**: Oats are commonly used in porridges and mueslis, while whole grain breads can be a base for various toppings.
- **Lunch and Dinner**: Barley and farro can be used in salads or soups to add texture and nutrition. Whole wheat pasta and breads are staples in Mediterranean cooking.
- **Snacks**: Whole grains like popcorn or whole grain crackers are excellent for snacking since they provide energy without the sugar spike and crash associated with refined snacks.

Cultural Significance

In Mediterranean cultures, whole grains are more than just food; they are a symbol of life and sustenance. Historically, grains were so valuable that they were used as a form of currency. Today, they continue to be a fundamental element of the Mediterranean diet, celebrated for their ability to nourish and sustain life.

By integrating whole grains into your daily meals, you can embrace a key component of the Mediterranean diet that supports not only physical health but also contributes to environmental sustainability. Whole grains' ability to provide sustained energy, improve overall health, and enhance meal satisfaction makes them an invaluable part of a balanced diet, truly living up to their role as a staple in one of the world's healthiest regions.

As we explore these essential ingredients, it becomes clear how they contribute not just to the longevity of the Mediterranean people but also offer a template for healthy eating that can be adapted worldwide. The simplicity and accessibility of these ingredients allow us to bring the spirit of the Mediterranean into our kitchens, helping us to embrace a diet centered around natural flavors, nutritional richness, and the joys of eating wholesomely.

Chapter 4:

Cooking Techniques of the Mediterranean Blue Zones

The Mediterranean diet is as much about how the food is prepared as it is about the ingredients themselves. The cooking techniques adopted in the Mediterranean Blue Zones not only enhance the natural flavors of the ingredients but also maximize their health benefits, preserving the essential nutrients while creating dishes that are both nourishing and delightful. This chapter explores some of the key cooking methods that define Mediterranean cuisine, illustrating how these techniques contribute to the longevity of the region's inhabitants.

4.1 Grilling and Roasting: Enhancing Flavor with Minimal Ingredients

Grilling and roasting are revered techniques in Mediterranean culinary traditions, celebrated for their simplicity and the depth of flavor they impart to dishes. These methods are particularly effective because they use high heat to cook the food quickly and efficiently, which not only enhances the natural flavors but also preserves many of the nutrients that can be lost during longer cooking processes.

Grilling in the Mediterranean

Grilling is a quintessential Mediterranean technique used primarily for preparing fish and vegetables, which are both central to the diet's focus on heart health and overall wellness. The process of grilling applies direct heat to the food, creating a crispy, charred exterior while keeping the interior moist and tender. This method is especially beneficial for fish, as the high heat quickly seals in the flavors and the omega-3 fatty acids, which are essential for cardiovascular health and cognitive function. Vegetables on the grill, such as bell peppers, eggplants, zucchinis, and asparagus, acquire a rich, smoky flavor that transforms the simple act of eating vegetables into a more enticing and enjoyable experience. The grill marks add not only visual appeal but also a texture that enhances the sensory experience of the meal.

Roasting: A Versatile Technique

Roasting, on the other hand, involves cooking food in an oven at a high temperature, which allows the heat to surround the food, cooking it evenly on all sides. This method is particularly suited to root vegetables like carrots, potatoes, beets, and onions, which develop a deep, sweet flavor as their natural sugars caramelize in the high heat. Whole grains, such as farro and barley, can also be roasted to bring out a nutty, toasted flavor that adds complexity to their naturally subtle taste.

One of the advantages of roasting is that it requires minimal fat to cook effectively, making it a healthier choice. A light drizzle of high-quality olive oil, some fresh herbs, and a sprinkle of sea salt are often all that is needed to elevate the natural flavors of the roasted ingredients. The simplicity of this seasoning approach is in line with the Mediterranean ethos of using quality ingredients and letting their natural tastes shine through.

Cultural and Health Implications

Both grilling and roasting are deeply embedded in the food culture of the Mediterranean, where dining is not only about nourishment but also about enjoyment and sharing. These cooking methods allow the ingredients' true flavors to stand out, encouraging a diet that is rich in nutrients without relying on heavy sauces or complicated seasonings. The health benefits of these techniques are significant, contributing to a dietary pattern that supports longevity and reduces the risk of chronic diseases.

Moreover, these methods are reflective of the Mediterranean lifestyle, which values simplicity and sustainability. By using less fat and sugar and more high-heat techniques like grilling and roasting, the cuisine naturally aligns with health guidelines that recommend a lower intake of saturated fats and added sugars, further proving that delicious food can also be healthful.

In sum, grilling and roasting are more than just cooking techniques in the Mediterranean—they are a celebration of the region's abundant natural produce and a testament to a culinary tradition that has mastered the art of healthy eating. These methods exemplify how simple preparations can lead to rich flavors, making every meal not only a nourishing experience but also a delightful one.

4.2 Simmering and Braising: Slow-Cooked Comfort Foods

Simmering and braising, deeply rooted in the culinary traditions of the Mediterranean, are cherished for their ability to infuse deep, rich flavors into simple ingredients. These methods exemplify a philosophy where food is treated with patience and reverence, allowing for the development of dishes that are not only comforting but also layered with taste and nourishment.

The Art of Simmering

Simmering is a gentle, slow cooking process that does wonders for a variety of dishes, particularly soups and stews. This technique involves cooking food at a temperature just below the boiling point, where small bubbles slowly surface. It is a method favored for its ability to blend and enhance flavors without the harshness of boiling, which can diminish the subtlety of the ingredients' natural tastes. In Mediterranean cooking, simmering is integral to preparing timeless recipes such as the hearty Greek fasolada, a bean soup that epitomizes the wholesome simplicity of the region's cuisine, or the Sardinian minestrone, a vegetable-rich soup that varies by season and what the garden offers, reflecting the Mediterranean's deep connection to its environment.

The slow cooking allows for the ingredients' flavors to meld in a way that each spoonful tastes complete and satisfying. Vegetables, beans, and herbs gently release their flavors into the broth, creating a base that is rich in nutrients and antioxidants, while the slow interaction of ingredients ensures that their health benefits are preserved and enhanced.

The Craft of Braising

Braising combines two cooking methods: a quick sear at high heat followed by a slow, gentle simmer in a minimal amount of liquid. This technique is particularly well-suited for tougher cuts of meat, which benefit from the long, slow cooking process that breaks down fibers and tenderizes the meat while infusing it with moisture and flavor. The initial searing locks in flavors and adds a caramelized crust that enhances the final dish's texture and taste.

In Mediterranean dishes, braising is not just a cooking method but a transformative process that turns simple ingredients like lamb, pork, and beef into tender, flavorful meals that are both nutritious and filling. The liquid used for braising often includes a mix of broth, wine, and herbs, which reduces to a rich, savory sauce that complements the main ingredients perfectly.

Cultural and Health Implications

Both simmering and braising reflect the Mediterranean lifestyle's slower pace, where cooking is as much about nourishing the soul as it is about feeding the body. These techniques encourage a mindful approach to food, where dishes are prepared thoughtfully and consumed leisurely, often surrounded by family and friends. The health benefits of these cooking methods are profound, as they preserve and often amplify the nutritional profile of the foods prepared.

Simmered and braised dishes are staples in Mediterranean homes, not only for their delicious flavors but also for their ability to bring people together. The comfort found in a bowl of slowly simmered soup or a tender braise is a testament to the region's understanding of how food can influence well-being, promote health, and enhance the quality of life.

By embracing these traditional cooking methods, one can experience the essence of Mediterranean cooking and its celebrated approach to longevity—a perfect blend of flavor, tradition, and health.

4.3 Marinating and Pickling: Preserving Freshness and Flavor

In the Mediterranean, the traditions of marinating and pickling are not just about extending the life of foods but also about enhancing flavors in creative ways. These age-old preservation techniques transform simple ingredients into complex, mouthwatering additions to any meal. Beyond just preventing spoilage, marinating and pickling are integral to bringing out the natural flavors in food, adding depth and a distinctive character that speaks to the Mediterranean's culinary heritage.

Marinating: Infusing Layers of Flavor

Marinating involves soaking foods in a seasoned liquid mixture for a specified period, which allows the flavors to penetrate deeply into the food. Marinades often include olive oil, vinegar or lemon juice, garlic, and a mix of herbs and spices, which infuse the food with vibrant tastes.

- **Tenderizing Effect**: The acids in marinades break down proteins and tenderize meats, making them succulent and juicy. Fish and poultry particularly benefit from this method, as the acids help to soften the fibers and allow the herbs and spices to soak in, resulting in moist and flavorful dishes.
- **Flavor Enhancement**: Mediterranean marinades are carefully crafted to highlight regional flavors, with common ingredients like oregano, rosemary, thyme, and citrus zest. The combination of these elements provides layers of flavor that make even simple ingredients shine.
- **Health Benefits**: Marinating before cooking, especially grilling, can reduce the formation of potentially harmful compounds caused by high-heat cooking. The antioxidants in herbs and spices like rosemary and garlic help neutralize these compounds, offering additional protection.

Pickling: A Tangy Burst of Taste

Pickling involves preserving vegetables, fruits, or even seafood in an acidic solution or brine, creating an environment that naturally prevents bacterial growth. The tangy flavor imparted by pickling complements many Mediterranean dishes, adding brightness and contrast to rich flavors.

- **Preservation Power**: Pickling extends the shelf life of foods, particularly seasonal produce, making them available long after their harvest period. This was essential for past generations and continues to be a sustainable practice today.
- **Probiotic Benefits**: Traditional pickling creates an environment for natural fermentation, which produces probiotics beneficial for gut health. Foods like pickled cucumbers and olives are rich in live cultures that promote a balanced digestive system.
- **Taste and Texture**: The sharp tang of pickled foods contrasts beautifully with the mild, rich flavors of Mediterranean staples like cheeses and meats. Pickled vegetables like artichokes, peppers, and cucumbers are often served as appetizers or garnishes, adding a crunchy, bright burst of flavor that enhances the dining experience.

Cultural and Culinary Value

Both marinating and pickling have deep cultural roots in the Mediterranean, where the art of preserving is as much about tradition as it is about flavor. These techniques have been passed down through generations, each family adding their own touch to the recipe. They exemplify the Mediterranean ethos of making the most of the land's bounty and using minimal ingredients to achieve exceptional results.

By incorporating marinating and pickling into your cooking repertoire, you can embrace a bit of Mediterranean heritage and introduce complex flavors that enrich your meals. Whether it's the subtle tenderness of marinated chicken or the tangy crunch of pickled peppers, these methods ensure your dishes are bursting with taste and packed with health benefits.

Chapter 5:

Breakfasts in the Blue Zones: Energizing Morning Meals

Breakfast in the Blue Zones is more than just the first meal of the day; it is a vital foundation for sustained energy and long-term health. In the Mediterranean, breakfast is treated with the same importance as any other meal, carefully composed to include nutrient-rich ingredients that set the tone for a day full of vitality. This chapter explores how traditional morning meals from regions like Greece, Sardinia, and Ikaria not only delight the palate but also provide the essential nutrients needed to support a lifestyle of longevity and wellness.

5.1 Greek Yogurt Parfait with Honey and Walnuts

Begin your day with a dish that encapsulates the essence of Mediterranean simplicity and luxury: the Greek Yogurt Parfait with Honey and Walnuts. This breakfast option is not only easy to prepare but also rich in essential nutrients that support a healthy start to the day.

Ingredients and Health Benefits

- **Greek Yogurt**: At the heart of this parfait is Greek yogurt, celebrated for its thick, creamy texture and high protein content. Protein is crucial for repairing tissues and maintaining muscle mass, making Greek yogurt an excellent breakfast choice. Additionally, Greek yogurt contains probiotics, which are beneficial for digestive health and maintaining a healthy gut microbiome.
- **Honey**: Drizzled over the yogurt, honey not only sweetens the dish but also introduces a range of antioxidants. These compounds help combat oxidative stress in the body, reducing inflammation and promoting overall health. Honey also provides a quick source of energy to start the day, making it a natural sweetener with benefits far surpassing mere taste.
- **Walnuts**: Adding both texture and nutritional value, walnuts are a superb source of omega-3 fatty acids, known for their role in promoting heart health and cognitive function. The crunch of walnuts offers a delightful contrast to the smooth yogurt, creating a satisfying sensory experience. They also contribute healthy fats that help absorb fat-soluble vitamins and provide sustained energy.

Culinary Delight

To assemble the parfait, begin by spooning a layer of Greek yogurt into a glass or bowl. Follow this with a layer of honey, ensuring it seeps into the yogurt for a touch of sweetness in every bite. Sprinkle a handful of chopped walnuts on top, adding not just crunch but also a nutty flavor that complements the mild tang of the yogurt. For those who enjoy a bit of extra texture and flavor, adding fresh fruits like berries or sliced bananas can elevate the dish further, introducing additional vitamins and fiber.

Serving Suggestions

This Greek Yogurt Parfait is perfect as a stand-alone breakfast or can be served as part of a larger brunch spread. It pairs beautifully with a cup of freshly brewed coffee or a glass of cold-pressed orange juice. For an added indulgence, a small sprinkle of cinnamon or a few drops of vanilla extract can be added to the yogurt before layering, enhancing the dish's flavor complexity.

Not only is the Greek Yogurt Parfait with Honey and Walnuts a healthful way to start the day, but it also embodies the Mediterranean lifestyle—focusing on high-quality, nutritious ingredients, prepared simply yet thoughtfully. This breakfast treats the body to a nourishing start, ensuring energy levels are balanced throughout the morning and setting the tone for a productive day.

5.2 Sardinian Frittata with Fresh Herbs and Tomatoes

A staple in Sardinian cuisine, the frittata is celebrated for its versatility and the ease with which it integrates fresh, local ingredients. This Sardinian Frittata with Fresh Herbs and Tomatoes is a perfect example of Mediterranean simplicity at its finest, turning everyday ingredients into a delightful meal that nourishes both the body and soul.

Ingredients and Their Benefits

- **Eggs**: The foundation of any frittata, eggs are a powerhouse of nutrition, providing high-quality protein which is crucial for muscle repair and growth. They also offer vitamins such as B12, D, and E, and minerals like zinc and iron, making them an excellent start to the day.
- **Fresh Herbs**: Herbs like basil, parsley, and mint are not just garnishes in this dish; they play a central role. These herbs add not only vibrant flavors but also a host of health benefits, including anti-inflammatory properties and significant amounts of antioxidants which protect the body against free radicals.
- **Tomatoes**: Adding a burst of color and moisture, tomatoes are rich in vitamin C, potassium, folate, and vitamin K. They are also

one of the best natural sources of lycopene, an antioxidant known for its cardiovascular benefits and cancer-preventing potentials.

Cooking Technique

To make a Sardinian Frittata, start by sautéing finely chopped onions and garlic in olive oil until they are translucent—a process that releases their sweet flavors. Add the chopped fresh herbs and diced ripe tomatoes, cooking them just long enough to soften them slightly. The eggs, beaten and seasoned with a pinch of salt and pepper, are then poured over the vegetables. The mixture is cooked gently on the stove top until the eggs are just set on the bottom and then finished under a broiler to achieve a lightly browned and fluffy top.

Flavor Profile

The result is a frittata that is tender and moist, with each bite infused with the herbal freshness of the garden and the sweet, tangy flavor of tomatoes. The eggs' subtle richness is a perfect backdrop for the bold flavors of the herbs and the acidity of the tomatoes, creating a balanced dish that is both hearty and light.

Serving Suggestions

This frittata is ideal for a leisurely weekend breakfast or a quick weekday brunch. It can be served hot directly from the oven or enjoyed at room temperature, making it a flexible option for any meal. Pair it with a rustic whole grain bread, a simple arugula salad dressed with lemon and olive oil, and a glass of crisp white wine or sparkling water for a truly Mediterranean dining experience.

Embracing the Sardinian way of cooking, this frittata celebrates the region's culinary traditions and its commitment to fresh, wholesome ingredients. It's a testament to the idea that simple cooking can be exceptionally satisfying and delicious, providing a meal that is both comforting and nutritious.

5.3 Ikarian Oatmeal with Dates and Almonds

Oatmeal is more than just a common breakfast; in Ikaria, it embodies a meal designed to support longevity and vitality, reflecting the local lifestyle that values slow mornings and nourishing ingredients. The inclusion of dates and almonds transforms ordinary oatmeal into an extraordinary dish, enhancing both its flavor and nutritional profile.

Nutritional Highlights

- **Oatmeal**: A fantastic source of soluble fiber, particularly beta-glucan, oatmeal helps lower cholesterol levels and stabilizes blood glucose levels. Its high fiber content also promotes a feeling of fullness, aiding in weight management by preventing overeating.

- **Dates**: These naturally sweet fruits are not only delicious but also packed with energy. Dates are high in fiber, which aids in digestion, and they're loaded with essential nutrients like potassium and magnesium, which contribute to heart health. Their natural sugars provide a quick energy boost, making them an ideal ingredient for a breakfast designed to energize.
- **Almonds**: Almonds bring a delightful crunch to the oatmeal, along with a wealth of health benefits. They are rich in healthy monounsaturated fats, protein, and vitamin E, an antioxidant that protects cells from oxidative damage. Almonds also contribute magnesium, which helps in muscle function and energy production.

Culinary Preparation

To prepare Ikarian Oatmeal with Dates and Almonds, start by cooking the oatmeal in water or a milk of choice until it reaches a creamy consistency. During the last few minutes of cooking, stir in chopped dates, which will soften slightly and infuse the oatmeal with their natural sweetness. Once the oatmeal is ready, top it with a generous sprinkle of chopped almonds for added texture and a boost of healthy fats.

Flavor and Texture

The combination of the soft, sweet dates with the crunchy, nutty almonds provides a satisfying contrast in textures that makes each spoonful interesting and enjoyable. The natural sweetness of the dates means there is no need for added sugars, making this a wholesome dish that is both nutritious and indulgent.

Serving Suggestions

Serve this oatmeal hot, with a drizzle of honey or maple syrup if extra sweetness is desired. For a creamier texture, a dollop of Greek yogurt or a splash of almond milk can be added on top. This dish can be beautifully paired with a cup of herbal tea or a fresh juice, completing a balanced, health-promoting breakfast that encapsulates the dietary wisdom of Ikaria.

This Ikarian Oatmeal with Dates and Almonds is not just a meal; it's a nourishing experience that supports a lifestyle focused on health and longevity. It demonstrates how a simple bowl of oatmeal can be transformed into a powerhouse of nutrition that fuels the body and delights the senses, embodying the principles of a Blue Zones diet.

Here are seven other Mediterranean-inspired breakfast recipes that reflect the healthful and flavorful traditions of the Blue Zones:

5.4 Sardinian Pane Carasau with Ricotta and Honey

Pane Carasau is a traditional Sardinian flatbread known for its paper-thin crispness and delightful texture. This ancient bread, often called "music bread" for its characteristic crackle when broken, serves as the perfect canvas for a light yet satisfying breakfast when paired with fresh ricotta cheese and a drizzle of local honey.

Ingredients and Their Benefits

- **Pane Carasau**: This crispy bread is made with just a few simple ingredients—wheat flour, water, yeast, and salt. It's baked until golden and crisp, providing a satisfying crunch that is both addictive and versatile.

- **Ricotta Cheese**: Ricotta adds a creamy, soft texture that contrasts beautifully with the crispness of the bread. It's rich in protein, which helps keep you feeling full throughout the morning, and provides calcium for bone health.

- **Honey**: Drizzling honey over the ricotta adds a natural sweetness that enhances the meal. Honey is not only delicious but also offers antioxidants and antibacterial properties.

Cooking Process

Pane Carasau can be purchased pre-made from specialty stores or online, which makes this breakfast both convenient and quick to assemble. To prepare, simply lay out a piece of the flatbread and spread a generous layer of fresh ricotta over the surface. The ricotta should be at room temperature to ensure it spreads easily and melds slightly into the bread.

Next, drizzle a good quality, preferably local, honey over the ricotta. The amount of honey can be adjusted according to taste, but a light drizzle usually suffices to add just the right touch of sweetness without overpowering the other flavors.

Flavor Profile

The combination of the nutty, earthy flavor of the Pane Carasau with the mild and slightly sweet ricotta creates a delightful base for the rich, floral notes of the honey. Each bite offers a contrast of textures from the crunchy bread to the creamy cheese, enhanced by the sticky sweetness of the honey.

Serving Suggestions

This dish is perfect on its own for a quick breakfast but can also be accompanied by a side of fresh fruit like figs, berries, or sliced peaches, which complement the flavors and add a refreshing element. For a more robust meal, it can be paired with a cup of Italian coffee or a herbal tea, making it a balanced and enjoyable morning treat.

Sardinian Pane Carasau with Ricotta and Honey is not only a testament to the simplicity of Italian cooking but also highlights how a few high-quality ingredients can come together to create a meal that is both nourishing and immensely satisfying. This breakfast option is ideal for those who appreciate the elegance of Italian cuisine and seek a light yet flavorful start to their day.

5.5 Ikarian Herbal Tea and Fig Bars

In Ikaria, a Greek island known for its impressive longevity rates, the local diet is a testament to the power of natural ingredients. Among these, herbal teas and figs play a crucial role, not only for their health benefits but also for their cultural significance. This breakfast pairing of Ikarian herbal tea and homemade fig bars captures the essence of the island's wholesome and natural eating habits.

Ingredients and Their Benefits

- **Herbal Tea**: Typically made from wild herbs like sage and thyme, Ikarian herbal tea is revered for its medicinal properties. Sage is known for its anti-inflammatory and antioxidant effects, while thyme can help improve immune function and has antibacterial properties.

- **Figs**: Figs are a natural source of dietary fiber, essential minerals such as magnesium, manganese, calcium, and vitamins, particularly K and B6. The natural sweetness of figs makes them a perfect ingredient in healthy snacks.

- **Nuts**: Commonly used nuts in these bars include almonds and walnuts, which are packed with healthy fats, proteins, and fiber. These nuts are heart-healthy and contribute to the feeling of fullness.

- **Honey**: As a natural sweetener, honey adds flavor without the spike in blood sugar levels associated with refined sugars. It also possesses antibacterial and antioxidant properties.

Cooking Process

Herbal Tea: To prepare the tea, boil water and steep the dried herbs—sage and thyme—for about 5-10 minutes. This allows the flavors and medicinal properties to infuse the water, creating a soothing, aromatic herbal tea.

Fig Bars: Start by chopping dried figs and nuts. Mix these with a binding agent like honey and perhaps a bit of oatmeal or whole grain flour to help hold the bars together. Press the mixture into a lined baking tray and bake at a low temperature until the bars are firm but not hard. Once cooled, cut the mixture into bar shapes.

Flavor Profile

The herbal tea offers a deeply soothing and aromatic experience, with the earthy tones of sage and thyme providing a calming effect. The fig bars are sweet and chewy, with a rich texture from the nuts and the natural moisture of the figs. The honey not only binds the ingredients but adds a touch of sweetness that complements the herbal notes of the tea.

Serving Suggestions

This combination is ideal for a slow morning, allowing time to savor the flavors and benefits of the meal. The fig bars can be enjoyed warm or at room temperature, and they pair beautifully with the herbal tea, creating a harmonious balance of sweet and earthy flavors. For an added touch, a slice of lemon or a sprig of fresh mint might be added to the tea for extra freshness.

Ikarian Herbal Tea and Fig Bars not only offer a nutritious start to the day but also embody the traditional dietary practices of Ikaria, showcasing how local ingredients can be used to create simple, healthful, and delicious meals. This breakfast choice is perfect for those looking to integrate the wisdom of

Blue Zones into their daily lives, promoting both longevity and pleasure.

5.6 Sardinian Pecorino and Pear Omelette

The Sardinian Pecorino and Pear Omelette is a delightful fusion of robust, sharp cheese and the gentle sweetness of pears, wrapped in a tender, fluffy egg mixture. This dish draws inspiration from Sardinia's rich pastoral traditions, showcasing the island's renowned Pecorino cheese, made from sheep's milk, alongside the natural sweetness of locally grown pears.

Ingredients and Their Benefits

- **Pecorino Cheese**: This hard, salty cheese is a staple in Sardinian cuisine and offers a depth of flavor as well as a good source of protein and calcium. Its sharpness beautifully contrasts with the subtle flavors in the dish.

- **Pears**: Adding a light, fruity sweetness, pears complement the intense flavor of the cheese and provide dietary fiber, vitamins, and natural sugars, making the omelette more balanced and palatable.

- **Eggs**: The base of the omelette, eggs are a perfect source of high-quality protein and essential nutrients that support overall health, including choline, which is important for brain function.

Cooking Process

To create this omelette, begin by whisking eggs in a bowl until they are smooth and slightly frothy, ensuring the omelette will be light and airy. Heat a non-stick skillet over medium heat and add a small amount of olive oil or butter to prevent sticking.

Pour the eggs into the skillet, and as they begin to set at the edges, gently pull them towards the center with a spatula, allowing the uncooked eggs to flow to the edges. Once the bottom is sufficiently set but the top is still slightly runny, arrange thin slices of pear and sprinkles of grated Pecorino cheese evenly over one half of the omelette.

Allow the cheese to melt slightly and the pears to warm through, then carefully fold the omelette in half, enclosing the filling. Let it cook for another minute to ensure the cheese is melted and the eggs are cooked through.

Flavor Profile

The Sardinian Pecorino and Pear Omelette offers a sophisticated blend of flavors. The sharp, salty taste of the Pecorino cheese pairs unexpectedly but deliciously with the sweet, almost floral notes of the pear. The eggs themselves are mild, fluffy, and serve as the perfect backdrop, allowing the filling to shine.

Serving Suggestions

This omelette is ideally served hot, straight from the pan. It can be accompanied by a simple side salad of mixed greens dressed with a balsamic vinaigrette or a slice of crusty Sardinian bread to mop up any creamy, cheesy residues. For a truly Sardinian experience, pair it with a glass of light, crisp white wine that complements the richness of the omelette.

The Sardinian Pecorino and Pear Omelette is not only a testament to the island's pastoral culinary traditions but also offers a breakfast or brunch option that is both nourishing and indulgent. This dish is a perfect example of how simple ingredients, when paired thoughtfully, can create a meal that is both satisfying and sophisticated.

5.7 Ikarian Honeyed Yogurt with Pistachios

This dish exemplifies the simplicity and health focus of Ikarian cuisine, blending the creamy texture of Greek yogurt with the natural sweetness of honey and the crunch of pistachios. It's a breakfast that offers a balance of protein, healthy fats, and the antioxidant properties of honey, all of which are essential for a nourishing start to the day.

Ingredients and Their Benefits

- **Greek Yogurt**: The base of this dish, Greek yogurt is celebrated for its rich, creamy texture and high protein content, which helps in muscle repair and satiety. It is also a good source of probiotics, beneficial bacteria that support gut health.

- **Honey**: Known for its antioxidant qualities, honey adds a natural sweetness without the spike in blood sugar associated with refined sugars. It also boasts antibacterial properties, contributing to overall health.

- **Pistachios**: These nuts are not only crunchy and flavorful but also packed with healthy fats, fiber, and antioxidants. They contribute to heart health and provide a satisfying crunch that contrasts beautifully with the creamy yogurt.

Cooking Process

To assemble the Ikarian Honeyed Yogurt with Pistachios, start by selecting a high-quality, plain

Greek yogurt. Opt for a full-fat version to enjoy its rich texture and full benefits, including increased satiety and a better flavor profile.

1. **Preparation of Yogurt**:
    - Spoon the Greek yogurt into a serving bowl. The amount can vary based on personal preference, but typically, a half to one cup serves as a good portion for one individual.
2. **Adding Honey**:
    - Drizzle a generous amount of local honey over the yogurt. The honey not only sweetens the yogurt but also infuses it with its delicate floral notes. The amount of honey can be adjusted according to taste, but starting with a tablespoon is recommended to achieve the perfect balance of sweetness without overpowering the yogurt.
3. **Incorporating Pistachios**:
    - Sprinkle shelled, unsalted pistachios over the top of the honeyed yogurt. You might choose to chop the pistachios lightly to release more of their oils and enhance their flavor. The pistachios add not only a

textural contrast but also a nutty flavor that complements the sweetness of the honey.

Flavor Profile

The resulting dish strikes a delightful balance between the creamy, tangy flavor of the yogurt and the sweet, floral notes of the honey. The pistachios provide a crunchy texture that contrasts with the smoothness of the yogurt, adding a layer of complexity to each bite. This combination of textures and flavors makes the Ikarian Honeyed Yogurt with Pistachios not only a healthful choice but also a culinary delight.

Serving Suggestions

This dish is perfect as a standalone breakfast or as part of a larger brunch spread. It pairs well with fresh fruits, such as berries or sliced peaches, which can be added to the bowl for extra freshness and a boost of vitamins. For a heartier meal, it can be served alongside whole-grain toast or a small bowl of granola.

The Ikarian Honeyed Yogurt with Pistachios embodies the principles of a Mediterranean diet—simple preparations, fresh ingredients, and flavors that not only satisfy the palate but also nourish the body. This breakfast is an excellent way to start the day, ensuring energy levels are maintained and the body receives a good balance of nutrients essential for health and longevity.

5.8 Sardinian Tomato and Basil Bruschetta

Sardinian Tomato and Basil Bruschetta is a quintessential Mediterranean appetizer that showcases the simplicity and freshness of Sardinian cuisine. This dish combines ripe tomatoes, aromatic basil, and high-quality extra virgin olive oil atop toasted slices of traditional Sardinian bread, creating a perfect harmony of flavors that is both refreshing and satisfying.

Ingredients and Their Benefits

- **Sardinian Bread**: Typically a dense, dry bread known as "pane carasau" or "music bread," which provides a crisp texture that holds up well under the juicy tomatoes and is perfect for toasting.
- **Ripe Tomatoes**: The star of the dish, ripe tomatoes are rich in vitamins C and K, potassium, folate, and lycopene, an antioxidant known for its cardiovascular benefits and cancer-prevention properties.

- **Fresh Basil**: Adds a fragrant, herbal note to the bruschetta, enhancing the dish with its fresh green aroma and flavor, while also offering anti-inflammatory properties.
- **Extra Virgin Olive Oil**: Drizzled over the top, it brings a fruity, peppery dimension to the dish and contributes healthy fats that are heart-healthy and promote good cholesterol levels.

Cooking Process

1. **Prepare the Bread**:
    - Begin by slicing the Sardinian bread into fairly thick slices. Toast these slices either in a toaster until they are just golden and crispy or under a broiler for a more authentic charred flavor.
2. **Mix the Topping**:
    - While the bread is toasting, prepare the tomato topping. Choose firm, perfectly ripe tomatoes for the best flavor and dice them into small, even pieces. Combine the chopped tomatoes in a bowl with freshly torn basil leaves, a pinch of salt, and a dash of pepper.
3. **Assemble the Bruschetta**:

- Once the bread is toasted to your liking, rub each slice with a clove of garlic for an extra layer of flavor—this step is optional but traditional.

- Spoon generous amounts of the tomato and basil mixture onto each slice of bread. Ensure each piece is well-covered and the juices start to soak slightly into the bread.

4. **Finishing Touches**:

    - Finally, drizzle each piece of bruschetta with high-quality extra virgin olive oil. This not only adds flavor but also helps to meld the flavors together.

Flavor Profile

The combination of the sweet and slightly acidic tomatoes with the aromatic basil and the rich, fruity olive oil on top of the crunchy, toasted bread creates a delightful array of textures and flavors. Each bite is a burst of freshness, with the olive oil rounding out the experience with its smooth and velvety finish.

Serving Suggestions

Sardinian Tomato and Basil Bruschetta is typically served as an appetizer or a snack, but it can also be a light, refreshing breakfast or brunch option. It pairs beautifully with various cheeses, cured meats, and a glass of crisp Sardinian white wine, such as Vermentino, which complements the fresh flavors of the bruschetta perfectly.

This dish not only encapsulates the essence of Sardinian cooking but also provides a healthy, vibrant start to any meal, emphasizing the Mediterranean's celebrated culinary traditions and their focus on health and longevity.

5.9 Ikarian Wild Green Pie (Hortopita)

Ikarian Wild Green Pie, known locally as Hortopita, embodies the essence of Ikaria's gastronomic culture—a cuisine deeply rooted in the use of wild, natural ingredients. This savory pie is a celebration of foraged greens and herbs, combined with the rich flavors of feta cheese, all encased in a light, flaky pastry. It's a traditional dish that reflects the island's reliance on locally sourced, nutrient-rich foods that contribute to the longevity of its residents.

Ingredients and Their Benefits

- **Foraged Greens**: Typically includes a variety of wild greens such as dandelion, spinach, nettles, and chard. These greens are not only abundant in fiber but are also packed with vitamins A, C, K, and minerals like iron and calcium, which are essential for maintaining healthy blood and bones.

- **Herbs**: Fresh herbs like mint, dill, and parsley are added for their flavor and health benefits, including digestive and anti-inflammatory properties.
- **Feta Cheese**: Provides a creamy, tangy contrast to the greens and adds calcium and protein, which are vital for bone health and muscle maintenance.
- **Phyllo Pastry**: The thin layers of pastry keep the dish light and provide a satisfying crunch when baked, making it a perfect vessel for the hearty filling.

Cooking Process

1. **Prepare the Greens**:
    - Rinse the greens thoroughly to remove any dirt or grit. Chop them coarsely and sauté in a pan with a little olive oil until they wilt down. This not only softens the greens but also intensifies their flavors.
2. **Mix the Filling**:
    - In a large bowl, mix the cooked greens with chopped herbs and crumbled feta

cheese. Season with salt, pepper, and a pinch of nutmeg to enhance the flavors. Some cooks also add a bit of beaten egg to the mixture to help bind the ingredients.

3. **Assemble the Pie**:

    - Lay out the phyllo pastry sheets, brushing each sheet lightly with olive oil before layering another on top. This helps to create a flaky texture once baked. Place the green and cheese mixture on the phyllo in the center, then fold the edges over or cover with another layer of phyllo, sealing the edges to keep the filling contained.

4. **Bake the Pie**:

    - Bake in a preheated oven at 375°F (190°C) until the pastry is golden and crisp, usually about 30-40 minutes. The high heat ensures that the pastry cooks through while the edges get nicely browned and crispy.

Flavor Profile

Ikarian Wild Green Pie offers a delightful mix of earthy and tangy flavors. The wild greens provide a slightly bitter undertone, beautifully balanced by the salty, creamy feta, and the fresh, aromatic herbs add a burst of brightness. The phyllo pastry adds a neutral but buttery crispness that encapsulates the filling, making each bite a perfect blend of textures and flavors.

Serving Suggestions

Hortopita can be served warm or at room temperature, making it a versatile dish for any meal. It's perfect as a main course, accompanied by a simple salad, or as a side dish in a larger meal. For a true Ikarian experience, pair it with a glass of local wine or herbal tea.

This dish is not just a treat for the palate but also a heart-healthy option that reflects the dietary habits of one of the world's renowned Blue Zones, where food is both a pleasure and a pathway to good health.

5.10 Sardinian Artichoke and Mint Frittata

The Sardinian Artichoke and Mint Frittata is a culinary delight that beautifully captures the essence of Sardinia's vibrant and seasonal cuisine. This dish combines the tender, earthy flavor of fresh artichokes with the refreshing zing of mint, all held together by a light and fluffy egg mixture. It's a simple yet sophisticated dish that highlights the island's tradition of utilizing fresh, local ingredients.

Ingredients and Their Benefits

- **Artichokes**: One of the stars of this dish, artichokes are not only delicious but also packed with nutrients. They are a fantastic source of fiber, vitamin C, and vitamin K, as well as antioxidants that help support liver health and reduce inflammation.

- **Mint**: Adds a fresh, aromatic flavor that lifts the dish. Mint is known for its digestive benefits, helping to soothe indigestion and inflammation.

- **Eggs**: Provide a high-quality protein that binds the frittata, making it filling and nutritious. Eggs are also a good source of B vitamins, essential for energy production.

Cooking Process

1. **Prepare the Artichokes**:
    - Clean and trim the artichokes by removing the tough outer leaves and slicing off the tops. Cut them into thin slices and immerse in water with a little lemon juice to prevent browning.

2. **Cook the Artichokes**:
    - Drain the artichokes and sauté them in a skillet with a little olive oil until they are

tender and slightly caramelized. This not only enhances their natural sweetness but also softens them for the frittata.

3. **Prepare the Frittata Mixture**:

    - In a large bowl, whisk together eggs, a pinch of salt, and freshly ground black pepper. Add freshly chopped mint leaves to the eggs, infusing them with flavor.

4. **Combine and Cook**:

    - Add the cooked artichokes to the egg mixture, ensuring they are evenly distributed. Pour the entire mixture back into the skillet, cooking over medium heat. As the edges begin to set, use a spatula to gently lift them, allowing the uncooked egg to flow underneath.

5. **Finish Cooking**:

    - Once the bottom is set and golden, place the skillet under a preheated broiler for a few minutes until the top of the frittata is firm and lightly browned.

Flavor Profile

The combination of artichokes and mint in this frittata creates a unique flavor profile. The artichokes provide a subtle, nutty earthiness which is brightened by the cool, peppery notes of mint. The eggs themselves are mild and creamy, providing a soft texture that complements the more pronounced flavors of the fillings.

Serving Suggestions

This frittata can be served hot or at room temperature, making it a versatile option for any meal—from a hearty breakfast to a light lunch or as part of a larger dinner spread. It pairs beautifully with a crisp, dry white wine or a sparkling water with lemon. For a complete meal, serve alongside a mixed green salad dressed with olive oil and balsamic vinegar, or with a selection of other Mediterranean dishes for a more elaborate feast.

The Sardinian Artichoke and Mint Frittata is not just a dish; it's a celebration of Sardinia's abundant natural produce, crafted into a meal that is both nourishing and immensely satisfying.

These breakfasts from the Blue Zones are not just meals but are also a reflection of a lifestyle that values longevity, health, and the enjoyment of every bite. By starting the day with these energizing meals, one can embrace the dietary habits that have supported some of the world's longest-lived populations.

Chapter 6:

Mediterranean Lunches: Wholesome Midday Meals

Lunches in the Mediterranean Blue Zones are not just about satisfying hunger—they are a celebration of fresh, seasonal ingredients and the region's long-standing tradition of sharing meals with family and friends. Midday meals are designed to be nourishing, light, and filled with flavors that reflect the diverse landscapes of Greece, Sardinia, and Ikaria. This chapter introduces three quintessential Mediterranean lunches that highlight the health-promoting simplicity of this diet. Each dish is crafted to fuel the body with balanced nutrition, while also providing an enriching, sensory experience that can be savored and shared.

6.1 Greek Salad with Feta Cheese and Kalamata Olives

The Greek Salad with Feta Cheese and Kalamata Olives is more than just a dish; it is a vibrant celebration of the Mediterranean's bounty. This salad is revered for its direct simplicity and the perfect balance of fresh ingredients that are staples in the healthy Mediterranean diet.

Nutritional Benefits

Each component of the Greek salad offers distinct health benefits:

- **Cucumbers**: High in water content, cucumbers help hydrate the body while providing a crisp texture.
- **Tomatoes**: A great source of vitamin C, potassium, folate, and vitamin K, tomatoes are also rich in lycopene, an antioxidant linked to many health benefits, including reduced risk of heart disease and cancer.
- **Bell Peppers**: These vegetables are loaded with vitamins A and C, which are antioxidants that enhance immune function and skin health.
- **Red Onions**: Known for their anti-inflammatory and antioxidant properties, they add not only a flavorful spice but also compounds like quercetin, which help combat chronic diseases.
- **Kalamata Olives**: A staple in Greek cuisine, these olives are high in monounsaturated fats and rich in antioxidants, contributing to heart health and longevity.
- **Feta Cheese**: Provides calcium, which is essential for bone health, and adds a creamy texture that contrasts beautifully with the crisp vegetables.

Culinary Experience

The assembly of the Greek Salad is straightforward, focusing on the freshness and quality of the ingredients. The cucumbers, tomatoes, and bell peppers are cut into hearty chunks that provide a satisfying crunch and allow each flavor to stand out. The red onions are thinly sliced, mitigating their sharpness and allowing them to mingle harmoniously with the other ingredients. Kalamata olives contribute a salty depth and a hint of luxury to the dish.

The salad is generously topped with crumbled feta cheese, which offers a creamy counterbalance to the crisp vegetables. This cheese's tangy flavor is a hallmark of Greek cuisine, providing a burst of richness with each bite.

Dressing and Serving

Dressing the salad is an exercise in subtlety; a drizzle of extra virgin olive oil and a squeeze of fresh lemon juice are all it takes to enhance the natural flavors. A sprinkle of dried oregano adds an aromatic touch that transports the eater to the Greek countryside.

This salad is typically served as a cool, refreshing starter or as a light main dish, perfect for warm days or as a nutritious addition to any meal. It pairs wonderfully with crusty bread or grilled meats, encapsulating the essence of a Mediterranean summer on a plate.

In conclusion, the Greek Salad with Feta Cheese and Kalamata Olives is not only a testament to the Mediterranean diet's health benefits but also a celebration of its flavors. It represents a lifestyle that values freshness, simplicity, and the joys of eating food that is both good and good for you.

6.2 Sardinian Minestrone Soup with Cannellini Beans and Kale

The Sardinian Minestrone Soup is a testament to the rustic, earthy flavors of Sardinian cuisine, which draws deeply from the island's agricultural heritage. This hearty soup encapsulates the essence of a Sardinian meal: simple, wholesome, and bursting with natural flavors.

Nutritional Composition

- **Cannellini Beans**: These beans are not only a rich source of plant-based protein but also provide dietary fiber which aids in digestion and helps maintain healthy blood sugar levels. Their creamy texture complements the broth's body, making the soup more satisfying.
- **Kale**: Chosen for its nutritional density, kale is loaded with vitamins A, K, C, and crucial minerals like manganese and calcium. It adds not only a vibrant green color but also a wealth

of nutrients that support overall health and well-being.

- **Root Vegetables**: Carrots, onions, and celery form the classic 'soffritto' that starts off the soup, building layers of flavor from the very beginning. These vegetables contribute essential vitamins and a natural sweetness that forms the base of the soup's complex flavor profile.

Flavor Profile

This Sardinian Minestrone is characterized by its robust and layered flavors. The cannellini beans and kale are simmered slowly with root vegetables, allowing all the ingredients to meld beautifully. Garlic adds depth and a pungent kick that is mellowed by the cooking process, while a medley of herbs such as rosemary, thyme, and a bay leaf infuse the soup with a subtle fragrance and freshness.

The use of kale introduces a mild bitterness that contrasts perfectly with the natural sweetness of the carrots and onions, creating a balanced flavor that is both rich and invigorating. The beans break down slightly, thickening the soup and giving it a hearty texture that is both fulfilling and comforting.

Preparation and Cooking

To prepare the soup, begin by sautéing the chopped onions, carrots, and celery in olive oil until they are soft and translucent. Add minced garlic and cook until fragrant. This foundation sets the stage for the rich flavors that follow. The cannellini beans, either pre-cooked or canned for convenience, are added along with a generous amount of vegetable broth or water. Once the soup reaches a boil, reduce the heat and let it simmer.

As the soup simmers, add the chopped kale and herbs, allowing them to cook down and meld their flavors with the base. The longer the soup cooks, the more the flavors develop and intensify. Season with salt and pepper to taste, and finish with a splash of extra virgin olive oil for an added layer of richness.

Serving Suggestions

Serve the Sardinian Minestrone hot, with a sprinkle of grated Parmesan cheese and a drizzle of extra virgin olive oil on top. It pairs wonderfully with a slice of crusty Sardinian bread, perfect for dipping into the flavorful broth. This soup not only provides a comforting meal on its own but can also be a fantastic starter for a larger, multi-course Sardinian feast.

The Sardinian Minestrone Soup with Cannellini Beans and Kale is a celebration of Sardinia's agricultural bounty, bringing warmth and nutrition in every spoonful. It embodies the Mediterranean principles of using fresh, local ingredients to create dishes that nourish both the body and the spirit.

6.3 Ikarian Lentil Stew with Vegetables and Herbs

Lentil stew is a staple in Ikaria, a Greek island known for its significant population of centenarians and their remarkable health and longevity. This Ikarian Lentil Stew with Vegetables and Herbs is a culinary reflection of the island's lifestyle, incorporating local, nutrient-rich ingredients cooked in a manner that maximizes their health benefits while delivering robust flavors.

Nutritional Highlights

- **Lentils**: A powerhouse of nutrition, lentils are rich in both protein and dietary fiber, which help to stabilize blood sugar levels and promote satiety. They also offer essential minerals such as iron and magnesium and B vitamins.
- **Vegetables**: The stew features a hearty mix of vegetables including carrots, which add sweetness and are high in beta-carotene, onions, which provide a base flavor and are rich in antioxidants, and tomatoes, known for their vitamin C and lycopene content.
- **Herbs**: Fresh Mediterranean herbs like oregano and parsley not only infuse the dish with flavors reminiscent of the Greek countryside but also contribute valuable anti-inflammatory and

antioxidant properties that support overall health.

Cooking Process

The preparation of this lentil stew begins with the sautéing of onions and garlic in olive oil until they are soft and translucent, setting the foundation for a flavorful dish. Carrots and tomatoes are then added, along with the lentils, and enough water or vegetable broth to cover. The stew is brought to a simmer, and the herbs are added, allowing their flavors to permeate throughout as the lentils and vegetables cook gently.

Flavor and Texture

As the stew simmers, the ingredients meld together, with the lentils absorbing the flavors of the herbs and vegetables while thickening the broth into a rich, comforting consistency. The herbs provide a fresh, aromatic quality that brightens the earthy taste of the lentils and the natural sweetness brought by the carrots and onions.

Health Benefits

This dish exemplifies the Ikarian approach to eating, which emphasizes legumes and vegetables as the cornerstone of the diet. The fiber from the lentils and vegetables helps improve digestive health, while the protein content supports muscle and bone health. The antioxidants and anti-inflammatory compounds from the herbs aid in reducing chronic disease risks, aligning with the dietary habits that contribute to the longevity of Ikaria's residents.

Serving Suggestions

Serve the Ikarian Lentil Stew warm, ideally with a piece of crusty whole-grain bread to soak up the delicious broth. A drizzle of extra virgin olive oil and a sprinkle of fresh parsley before serving can enhance the flavors and add a touch of richness. This stew is perfect for a nourishing lunch that satisfies without being overly heavy, providing energy and vital nutrients to fuel the rest of the day.

In essence, the Ikarian Lentil Stew with Vegetables and Herbs is more than just a meal; it's a celebration of life's simplicity and the natural bounty that supports health and longevity. It invites one to slow down and enjoy the nourishing qualities of good food shared with loved ones.

6.4 Sardinian Pecorino and Fig Salad

This Sardinian Pecorino and Fig Salad combines the sharp, salty flavors of Pecorino cheese with the lush sweetness of fresh figs, set against a backdrop of peppery arugula and mixed greens. The addition of a honey-balsamic vinaigrette not only enhances the flavors but also melds them together into a harmonious dish that is as delightful to the palate as it is beautiful on the plate.

Ingredients and Their Benefits

- **Arugula and Mixed Greens**: These leafy greens form the base of the salad, providing essential nutrients such as vitamins A, C, and K, as well as calcium and iron. Arugula, known for its peppery flavor, adds a spicy note that contrasts nicely with the sweetness of the figs.
- **Sardinian Pecorino Cheese**: A hard, salty cheese that adds depth and a rich umami flavor to the salad. Pecorino is also a good source of protein and calcium.
- **Fresh Figs**: Soft, sweet, and full of fiber, potassium, and natural sugars, figs are the perfect counterbalance to the salty cheese and spicy greens.
- **Honey-Balsamic Vinaigrette**: A dressing that combines the sweetness of honey with the tart acidity of balsamic vinegar, enhancing the overall flavors of the salad while adding a slight tanginess that ties all the components together.

Cooking Process

1. **Prepare the Salad Base**:
    - Wash and dry the arugula and mixed greens thoroughly to ensure they are clean and crisp. Place them in a large salad bowl as the foundation of the dish.

2. **Add the Cheese and Figs**:
   - Slice the Sardinian Pecorino cheese into thin pieces or shave it with a vegetable peeler for a more delicate texture. Arrange the cheese over the greens.
   - Cut the fresh figs into quarters or slices, depending on their size, and distribute them evenly across the salad.
3. **Make the Vinaigrette**:
   - In a small bowl, whisk together equal parts of honey and balsamic vinegar, adding a stream of extra virgin olive oil while whisking to create an emulsion. Season with a pinch of salt and black pepper to taste.
4. **Dress the Salad**:
   - Drizzle the honey-balsamic vinaigrette over the salad just before serving to ensure the greens remain crisp and vibrant. Gently toss the salad to coat all the ingredients evenly with the dressing.

Flavor Profile

The Sardinian Pecorino and Fig Salad is a study in contrasts: the sharp, salty cheese pairs perfectly with the sweet, juicy figs, while the arugula provides a spicy undertone that complements both. The honey-balsamic vinaigrette ties these elements together with its sweet and tangy flavor, making each bite a complex and satisfying experience.

Serving Suggestions

This salad makes an excellent starter for a larger meal or can serve as a light lunch on its own. Pair it with a chilled glass of Vermentino or another crisp white wine from Sardinia for a truly regional dining experience. For a more substantial meal, consider serving it alongside a crusty loaf of Italian bread or as part of a larger spread featuring other Mediterranean dishes.

6.5 Ikarian Fisherman's Soup

The Ikarian Fisherman's Soup is a quintessential dish from the Greek island of Ikaria, renowned for its high longevity rates. This soup features a hearty blend of local seafood, embodying the island's maritime heritage and nutritional philosophy. Packed with omega-3 fatty acids and flavored with a medley of fresh herbs and vegetables, this soup is not only a healthful choice but also a comforting and satisfying meal.

Ingredients and Their Benefits

- **Variety of Fish and Shellfish**: Typically includes whatever the catch of the day might be, such as sea bass, snapper, and shellfish like mussels or clams. These ingredients are excellent sources of omega-3 fatty acids, which are crucial for cardiovascular health and cognitive function.

- **Tomatoes**: Add a rich, tangy base to the soup and are a great source of vitamin C, potassium, folate, and vitamin K.
- **Onions and Garlic**: Fundamental for flavor, both onions and garlic have anti-inflammatory properties and contribute to the overall heart health benefits of the dish.
- **White Wine**: A splash of white wine enhances the flavors of the seafood and adds a slight acidity that balances the richness of the fish.
- **Dill and Parsley**: These herbs are not just for garnish; dill adds a fresh, almost anise-like taste, while parsley offers a mild, clean flavor and provides additional antioxidants and vitamins.

Cooking Process

1. **Prepare the Seafood**:
    - Clean and prepare the fish and shellfish. If using whole fish, fillet them, or if preferred, leave them in larger chunks. Scrub shellfish under cold water and de-beard mussels if necessary.
2. **Sauté the Aromatics**:

- In a large pot, heat olive oil over medium heat. Add finely chopped onions and minced garlic, sautéing until they are translucent and fragrant. This provides a flavor base that will infuse the entire soup.

3. **Deglaze with Wine**:
   - Pour in a splash of white wine, scraping up any bits that have stuck to the bottom of the pot. Allow the wine to reduce slightly, which concentrates the flavor.

4. **Add Tomatoes and Simmer**:
   - Stir in chopped fresh tomatoes (canned tomatoes can also be used outside of tomato season). Let the mixture come to a gentle simmer, allowing the tomatoes to break down and form a rich, flavorful broth.

5. **Cook the Seafood**:
   - Add the prepared fish and shellfish to the pot. Cover and let the soup simmer gently. The fish should be cooked through but tender, and shellfish should open up, indicating they are done.

6. **Season and Serve**:
   - Finish the soup with chopped fresh dill and parsley, adding a layer of freshness to

the dish. Adjust seasoning with salt and freshly ground black pepper. Serve hot, with a drizzle of extra virgin olive oil on top and a side of crusty bread to soak up the flavorful broth.

Flavor Profile

Ikarian Fisherman's Soup offers a rich and complex taste experience. The freshness of the seafood shines through, complemented by the tangy tomato broth and aromatic herbs. The white wine provides a subtle depth and brightness that ties all the flavors together.

Serving Suggestions

This soup is perfect as a standalone meal or as part of a larger spread in a communal setting, which is typical in Ikarian culture. It pairs wonderfully with a crisp, dry white wine, such as a local Greek Assyrtiko, enhancing the light but rich flavors of the dish. Enjoy this warming soup with family and friends, embracing the Ikarian way of life that values both diet and community as essential ingredients to longevity.

6.6 Sardinian Pasta with Bottarga

Sardinian Pasta with Bottarga is a classic dish from the island of Sardinia, known for its robust flavors and simple, yet rich ingredients. Bottarga, the star of this dish, is cured fish roe that is typically grated or sliced thinly to top pasta, bringing with it a salty and briny flavor that is unique to this Mediterranean delicacy. This pasta dish encapsulates the essence of Sardinian cuisine, combining the deep umami of bottarga with the freshness of garlic and the warmth of chili flakes.

Ingredients and Their Benefits

- **Bottarga**: Made from mullet or tuna roe that has been salted, cured, and dried, bottarga is rich in omega-3 fatty acids, which are known for their heart health benefits and ability to reduce inflammation.
- **Spaghetti**: Serves as the perfect base, its neutral flavor allowing the bold tastes of the other ingredients to shine through.
- **Garlic**: Adds a pungent, aromatic depth to the dish, and is well known for its health benefits, including its ability to boost immune function and reduce blood pressure.
- **Olive Oil**: A staple in Mediterranean cooking, olive oil is used to sauté the garlic and to toss the pasta, adding a smooth, rich texture and healthy fats.
- **Chili Flakes**: Provide a gentle heat that cuts through the richness of the bottarga and enhances the overall flavor profile of the dish.

Cooking Process

1. **Prepare the Pasta**:

   - Cook the spaghetti in a large pot of salted boiling water according to package instructions until al dente. It's important to keep the pasta slightly firm as it will continue to cook when tossed with the sauce.

2. **Sauté Garlic**:

   - While the pasta cooks, heat a generous amount of olive oil in a large skillet over medium heat. Add thinly sliced or minced garlic and sauté just until it becomes fragrant and begins to turn golden. Be careful not to burn the garlic as it can become bitter.

3. **Add Bottarga and Chili Flakes**:

   - Lower the heat and add grated bottarga and a pinch of chili flakes to the garlic and oil. Stir to combine, allowing the flavors to meld. The bottarga will dissolve slightly, creating a rich, salty sauce.

4. **Toss the Pasta**:

   - Drain the pasta, reserving a cup of the pasta cooking water. Add the spaghetti directly to the skillet with the bottarga and garlic. Toss well to coat the pasta evenly. If the mixture seems dry, add a little of the reserved pasta water to help create a more cohesive sauce.

5. **Serve**:

    - Plate the pasta and give an extra sprinkle of bottarga on top for an additional burst of flavor. A drizzle of high-quality extra virgin olive oil can be added for richness.

Flavor Profile

Sardinian Pasta with Bottarga offers a potent combination of salty, briny, and spicy flavors. The bottarga provides a strong umami character, which is balanced by the fresh and slightly spicy notes from the garlic and chili flakes. The olive oil brings everything together, smoothing out the flavors into a harmonious dish.

Serving Suggestions

This dish is best served immediately while it's hot. It pairs beautifully with a light, crisp white wine such as Vermentino, which complements the saltiness of the bottarga without overpowering it. Simple green salads dressed with lemon and olive oil make a refreshing side to this rich pasta dish.

Sardinian Pasta with Bottarga is a true reflection of the island's culinary heritage, offering a taste of the sea in every bite and a satisfying experience that is both gourmet and straightforward.

6.7 Ikarian Chickpea and Spinach Salad

The Ikarian Chickpea and Spinach Salad is a vibrant and healthful dish that reflects the dietary principles found in one of the world's famous Blue Zones, Ikaria, Greece. This salad combines the hearty textures of chickpeas with the nutritional powerhouse of spinach, enhanced by the sharp flavors of red onion and feta cheese. It's a simple yet profoundly nutritious dish that exemplifies how the Ikarians integrate legumes and leafy greens into their diet, contributing to their renowned longevity and health.

Ingredients and Their Benefits

- **Chickpeas**: A staple in the Ikarian diet, chickpeas are a great source of plant-based protein, fiber, vitamins, and minerals which help in managing weight, controlling blood sugar levels, and supporting digestive health.
- **Spinach**: Loaded with vitamins A, C, K, iron, and antioxidants, spinach contributes to strong bones, improved eyesight, and a reduced risk of chronic diseases.

- **Red Onion**: Adds a sharp, slightly sweet flavor and brings anti-inflammatory and antioxidant properties to the dish.
- **Feta Cheese**: This tangy cheese not only adds flavor depth but also provides calcium, phosphorus, and protein, which are essential for bone health.
- **Olive Oil and Lemon Juice Dressing**: A simple dressing that complements the salad ingredients without overpowering them. Olive oil is renowned for its heart-healthy fats, while lemon juice provides a refreshing tang and vitamin C, enhancing iron absorption from the spinach.

Cooking Process

1. **Prepare the Chickpeas**:
    - If using dried chickpeas, soak them overnight, then boil until tender. For convenience, canned chickpeas can be used instead; just rinse and drain them to remove excess sodium.
2. **Wilt the Spinach**:
    - Quickly sauté fresh spinach leaves in a little olive oil just until they begin to wilt. This preserves their color and texture, ensuring they blend well with the other

salad components without becoming too soggy.

3. **Combine the Ingredients**:

    - In a large mixing bowl, combine the cooked chickpeas, wilted spinach, finely diced red onion, and crumbled feta cheese. Toss gently to mix the ingredients evenly.

4. **Dress the Salad**:

    - Whisk together extra virgin olive oil and fresh lemon juice with a pinch of salt and black pepper to taste. Drizzle this dressing over the salad and toss again to coat all ingredients well. The dressing will lightly marinate the ingredients, melding the flavors together beautifully.

5. **Chill and Serve**:

    - For the best flavor, let the salad sit for a few minutes before serving, allowing the flavors to integrate. This salad can be served chilled or at room temperature, making it versatile for various dining settings.

Flavor Profile

The Ikarian Chickpea and Spinach Salad is a delightful blend of textures and flavors. The creamy chickpeas, tender spinach, crunchy onions, and crumbly feta create a satisfying mouthfeel. The lemon dressing adds a fresh, zesty note that enhances the natural flavors of the vegetables and balances the richness of the feta.

Serving Suggestions

This salad is perfect as a standalone meal for a light lunch or can serve as a nutritious side dish at dinner. It pairs well with a slice of whole-grain bread or a serving of quinoa for a more filling meal. Given its health benefits and delicious taste, this salad is ideal for anyone looking to incorporate more plant-based, nutrient-dense foods into their diet in a flavorful way.

6.8 Sardinian Roasted Lamb with Rosemary and Garlic

The Sardinian Roasted Lamb with Rosemary and Garlic is a quintessential dish that embodies the rich culinary heritage of Sardinia, Italy. This recipe showcases the island's pastoral traditions, utilizing local ingredients like fresh rosemary, garlic, and sea salt to enhance the naturally robust flavors of lamb. Accompanied by roasted potatoes, this dish is not only a staple at Sardinian tables but also a celebration of simplicity and flavor.

Ingredients and Their Benefits

- **Lamb**: A traditional meat in Sardinian cuisine, lamb is valued for its high-quality protein, essential vitamins (B12), and minerals (zinc, iron). It's particularly noted for its rich, distinct flavor that pairs well with the aromatic herbs of the region.
- **Rosemary**: This aromatic herb is not just a flavor enhancer—rosemary is also known for its antioxidants and anti-inflammatory compounds, which can improve digestion and enhance memory and concentration.
- **Garlic**: Used both for its health benefits and its flavor, garlic adds depth to the dish and offers cardiovascular health benefits by helping to lower blood pressure and improve cholesterol levels.
- **Sardinian Sea Salt**: Harvested from the Mediterranean waters surrounding Sardinia, this sea salt contains traces of minerals like magnesium and potassium and enhances the natural flavors of the lamb.

Cooking Process

1. **Preparation of the Lamb**:
    - Begin by making a marinade with finely chopped rosemary, minced garlic, Sardinian sea salt, black pepper, and olive oil. Rub this mixture generously over the

lamb, covering all sides. Allow the lamb to marinate for at least an hour, or overnight in the refrigerator, to absorb the flavors.

2. **Roasting the Lamb**:
   - Preheat your oven to a moderate temperature (about 325°F or 165°C). Place the lamb in a roasting pan, and if desired, add a splash of white wine or broth to the pan for additional moisture and flavor. Cover with foil and roast, basting occasionally with its juices, until the lamb is tender and cooked to your preference.
3. **Preparing the Potatoes**:
   - While the lamb roasts, prepare the potatoes. Cut them into halves or quarters, depending on their size, and toss them with olive oil, rosemary, salt, and pepper. Arrange them around the lamb in the roasting pan about halfway through the cooking process so they absorb some of the lamb's flavors and become crispy.
4. **Final Steps**:
   - Once the lamb is cooked to your liking and the potatoes are golden and crispy, remove from the oven. Let the lamb rest for several minutes before slicing. This rest period allows the juices to redistribute

throughout the meat, ensuring it is juicy and flavorful when carved.

Flavor Profile

Sardinian Roasted Lamb with Rosemary and Garlic delivers a powerful taste experience. The lamb itself is succulent and rich, with the rosemary and garlic providing a fragrant and slightly pungent counterbalance that elevates the meat's natural flavors. The roasted potatoes serve as a hearty and comforting side that complements the meat's richness.

Serving Suggestions

Serve this dish as a centerpiece for a family gathering or festive occasion. It pairs beautifully with a robust Sardinian red wine, such as Cannonau, which complements the lamb's richness. For a complete meal, consider adding a side of steamed seasonal vegetables or a simple green salad dressed with olive oil and lemon.

This dish not only provides a delicious taste of Sardinian culinary tradition but also a wholesome meal that celebrates the island's bountiful produce and pastoral lifestyle.

6.9 Ikarian Wild Herb Pie

The Ikarian Wild Herb Pie is a celebration of the lush, verdant landscape of Ikaria, Greece, a region known for its impressive longevity rates. This savory pie encapsulates the essence of Ikarian cuisine, which heavily utilizes wild, foraged herbs and local produce. Filled with a fragrant blend of fennel, dill, mint, and enriched with creamy local goat cheese, this dish is not only a testament to the island's culinary traditions but also to its health-promoting diet.

Ingredients and Their Benefits

- **Foraged Herbs (Fennel, Dill, Mint)**: These herbs are staples in Ikarian cooking and are known for their health benefits. Fennel is rich in fiber and can help with digestion, dill has anti-inflammatory properties, and mint is excellent for soothing stomach issues and improving oral health.
- **Goat Cheese**: Typically lighter and easier to digest than cow's milk cheeses, goat cheese adds creaminess and a tangy flavor to the pie. It also provides protein, calcium, and essential fatty acids.
- **Thin Pastry**: Usually made from whole wheat flour, which adds a nutritious, fibrous element to the pie, holding the filling and adding a satisfying crunch.

Cooking Process

1. **Prepare the Herbs**:

- Wash and finely chop the herbs—fennel, dill, and mint. The key to maximizing their aromatic properties is to use them fresh and raw, just before assembling the pie to preserve their essential oils and flavors.

2. **Make the Pastry**:
   - Prepare a simple dough from whole wheat flour, a bit of olive oil, and water. Roll the dough out into a thin sheet, enough to cover the base and sides of your pie dish. Pre-bake the crust lightly in a preheated oven at 350°F (175°C) for about 10 minutes to achieve a semi-crisp texture that will hold the moist filling without becoming soggy.

3. **Combine the Filling**:
   - In a mixing bowl, blend the chopped herbs with crumbled goat cheese. Season with salt and pepper to taste. For an extra hint of flavor, you can add finely chopped onions or garlic, which complement the herbs beautifully.

4. **Assemble the Pie**:
   - Spread the herb and cheese mixture evenly over the pre-baked pastry base. If desired, layer some more herbs on top for added flavor and visual appeal.

5. **Bake the Pie**:
    - Cover the pie with another layer of thin pastry or leave it open-faced, which is traditional for some rustic Greek pies. Bake in the oven at 375°F (190°C) for about 20-25 minutes, or until the pastry is golden and the cheese is bubbly.

Flavor Profile

Ikarian Wild Herb Pie offers a unique blend of earthy and tangy flavors. The freshness of the herbs imparts a vibrant, almost anise-like flavor from the fennel, with dill providing a sweet and mint adding a cool aftertaste. The goat cheese enhances these flavors with its creamy texture and tangy bite, all enveloped in a crispy, hearty crust.

Serving Suggestions

This pie is perfect as a light lunch or a substantial snack. It pairs wonderfully with a fresh green salad dressed with olive oil and lemon, reflecting the simplicity and healthfulness of Ikarian eating habits. Enjoy this pie warm or at room temperature to fully appreciate its flavors.

Enjoying this pie not only means savoring a delicious meal but also embracing the dietary habits linked to the longevity of Ikaria's residents, making it a truly nourishing experience.

6.10 Sardinian Fava Bean and Pecorino Cheese Dip

The Sardinian Fava Bean and Pecorino Cheese Dip is a delightful culinary creation that showcases the rustic and wholesome flavors characteristic of Sardinian cuisine. Made from just a handful of locally-sourced ingredients, this dip offers a creamy texture and a rich flavor profile that highlights the natural tastes of each component. It's a versatile dish that serves as an excellent appetizer or a light lunch, perfect for spreading on crispy Sardinian pane carasau.

Ingredients and Their Benefits

- **Fava Beans**: These beans are a staple in Mediterranean diets, known for their high protein and fiber content, which can aid in digestion and provide a feeling of fullness. Fava beans are also rich in important nutrients like potassium, iron, and magnesium.
- **Pecorino Cheese**: A hard, salty cheese from Sardinia, made from sheep's milk. Pecorino is not only flavorful but also provides calcium and protein.
- **Olive Oil**: A cornerstone of Mediterranean cooking, olive oil is celebrated for its heart-

healthy monounsaturated fats and its ability to enhance the absorption of fat-soluble vitamins.

- **Lemon Zest**: Adds a fresh, citrusy burst that lifts the richness of the beans and cheese, providing vitamin C and an aromatic flavor.

Cooking Process

1. **Prepare the Fava Beans**:
    - If using dried fava beans, soak them overnight, then boil until they are soft and tender. Drain the beans and remove any tough outer skins for a smoother texture in the dip.
2. **Blend the Ingredients**:
    - In a food processor or blender, combine the cooked fava beans with grated Pecorino cheese, a generous drizzle of olive oil, and the zest of one lemon. Blend until the mixture reaches a creamy, smooth consistency. For a thinner dip, add a little more olive oil or a splash of water to achieve the desired texture.
3. **Season and Adjust**:
    - Taste the dip and adjust the seasoning as needed with salt (though Pecorino is quite salty on its own), cracked black pepper, and more lemon zest if desired. For an

extra layer of flavor, consider adding a clove of garlic or a handful of fresh herbs like parsley or mint during the blending process.

4. **Serve**:

    - Transfer the dip to a serving bowl. Drizzle with a little more olive oil and sprinkle with a bit of crushed red pepper flakes for color and a slight kick. Serve with pieces of pane carasau, the traditional Sardinian flatbread, which provides a delightful crunch contrasting the creamy texture of the dip.

Flavor Profile

This Sardinian Fava Bean and Pecorino Cheese Dip is wonderfully rich and creamy, with the earthiness of the fava beans beautifully complemented by the sharpness of the Pecorino cheese. The olive oil adds a smooth, velvety finish, while the lemon zest infuses a bright, refreshing note that cuts through the richness.

Serving Suggestions

This dip is perfect as part of a Mediterranean appetizer spread, accompanied by olives, cured meats, and other cheeses. It can also be served as a part of a simple lunch, alongside a salad and some fresh fruit for a balanced meal. Enjoy this dip with a glass of

Vermentino or another crisp white wine from Sardinia for a truly authentic regional experience.

The Sardinian Fava Bean and Pecorino Cheese Dip is not just a treat for the palate but also an expression of Sardinian culinary traditions, combining simple ingredients for maximum flavor and enjoyment.

These Mediterranean lunches are not only balanced and flavorful but also embody the Blue Zones principles of mindful, healthful eating. They demonstrate how simple ingredients can be transformed into wholesome, life-enhancing meals that nourish the body and uplift the spirit.

Chapter 7:

Dinners from the Blue Zones: Flavorful Evening Dishes

As the sun sets over the landscapes of the world's Blue Zones, families gather around the dinner table to enjoy meals that are not only delicious but also steeped in centuries-old traditions of health and longevity. This chapter delves into the evening meals that are central to the life-extending diets of regions like Ikaria, Greece, and Sardinia, Italy. Here, dinner is more than just a meal; it is a daily ritual that reinforces community bonds, relaxes the mind, and nourishes the body with whole, nutrient-rich ingredients. Explore a variety of dishes that exemplify how simple ingredients, when cooked with traditional methods and shared with loved ones, can lead to a healthier, longer life.

7.1 Grilled Fish with Lemon and Garlic from Ikaria

In Ikaria, Greece, grilling fish is more than a cooking method; it's a tradition that brings together fresh, local ingredients for a heart-healthy meal that epitomizes the island's approach to longevity. This simple yet elegant dish uses minimal ingredients—fresh fish, lemon, and garlic—to enhance the natural flavors of the seafood without overpowering it. Grilled Fish with Lemon and Garlic is a classic Ikarian dish, reflecting the island's abundant maritime resources and the dietary habits that contribute to the health and longevity of its inhabitants.

Ingredients and Their Benefits

- **Fresh Fish**: Typically, local varieties such as snapper, sea bream, or mackerel are used. These fish are rich in omega-3 fatty acids, which are crucial for cardiovascular health and reducing inflammation.
- **Lemon**: Adds a fresh, citrusy brightness to the fish, enhancing its flavor while providing vitamin C and aiding in digestion and detoxification.
- **Garlic**: Known for its health benefits, including its ability to boost the immune system and reduce heart disease risks, garlic adds a robust flavor that complements the fish beautifully.

Cooking Process

1. **Prepare the Fish**:
    - Start with fresh, cleaned whole fish or fillets. Make several diagonal slashes in the flesh of whole fish to ensure even cooking and flavor penetration.

2. **Marinate**:

    - In a small bowl, combine olive oil, freshly squeezed lemon juice, minced garlic, salt, and pepper. Brush this mixture generously over the fish, ensuring it gets into the slashes and cavity if using whole fish. Let it marinate for at least 30 minutes in the refrigerator.

3. **Prepare the Grill**:

    - Heat your grill to a medium-high temperature. Clean the grill grates and brush them with oil to prevent the fish from sticking.

4. **Grill the Fish**:

    - Place the fish on the grill, skin side down if using fillets. Grill the fish, turning once, until the skin is crisp and the flesh flakes easily with a fork. This usually takes about 4-7 minutes per side, depending on the thickness of the fish.

5. **Serve**:

    - Once cooked, transfer the fish to a serving plate. Serve with additional lemon wedges for squeezing and a sprinkling of fresh herbs, such as parsley or dill, for added flavor and a touch of color.

Flavor Profile

Grilled Fish with Lemon and Garlic offers a delightful blend of flavors that are both refreshing and satisfying. The lemon provides a tangy contrast to the rich, oily fish, while the garlic adds depth and warmth. The grilling process imparts a subtle smokiness and a pleasant char that enhances the overall taste.

Serving Suggestions

This dish can be served with a side of steamed vegetables, a fresh salad, or over a bed of whole grains like farro or quinoa for a balanced meal. Pair it with a crisp white wine, such as an Assyrtiko from Greece, to complement the flavors of the fish.

Grilled Fish with Lemon and Garlic is not only a delicious meal but also an integral part of the Ikarian diet, known for promoting health and longevity. It's a simple yet sophisticated dish that embodies the essence of Mediterranean cooking and the Blue Zone lifestyle.

7.2 Sardinian Seafood Pasta with Cherry Tomatoes and Basil

The Sardinian Seafood Pasta with Cherry Tomatoes and Basil is a quintessential Mediterranean dish that perfectly marries the freshness of the sea with the vibrant flavors of the garden. This pasta dish is not just a treat for the palate but also embodies the healthful eating habits of Sardinia, known for its high concentration of centenarians. It's a testament to how a few well-chosen ingredients can create a meal that's both nutritious and bursting with flavor.

Ingredients and Their Benefits

- **Seafood**: Typically includes a mix of shrimp, clams, and mussels, which are staples in Sardinian cuisine. Seafood is high in protein and omega-3 fatty acids, which are crucial for heart health and brain function.

- **Cherry Tomatoes**: These small, sweet tomatoes add a burst of flavor and color to the dish. They are rich in vitamins C and K, potassium, and antioxidants, particularly lycopene, which is known for its cardiovascular benefits.

- **Basil**: Fresh basil not only enhances the dish with its peppery and slightly sweet flavor but also provides anti-inflammatory and antibacterial properties.

- **Garlic and Olive Oil**: Fundamental elements in Mediterranean cooking, garlic and olive oil add depth and heart-healthy fats to the dish, enhancing both its flavor and nutritional profile.

Cooking Process

1. **Prepare the Seafood**:
    - Clean and prepare the seafood. For clams and mussels, ensure they are scrubbed and debearded. Shrimp should be peeled and deveined if not already prepared.
2. **Cook the Pasta**:
    - Boil a large pot of salted water and cook the pasta (spaghetti or linguine works well) just until al dente. Reserve a cup of pasta water for later use.
3. **Sauté the Aromatics**:
    - In a large skillet, heat olive oil over medium heat. Add minced garlic and sauté until fragrant, being careful not to burn it. Add cherry tomatoes and cook until they start to break down and release their juices.
4. **Add Seafood**:
    - Increase the heat to medium-high and add the prepared seafood to the skillet. If using

clams and mussels, cover the skillet and cook until they open (discard any that do not open). Add shrimp and cook until pink and opaque.

5. **Combine Pasta and Seafood**:

    - Toss the cooked pasta into the skillet with the seafood and tomatoes. Add a splash of reserved pasta water to help the sauce cling to the pasta. Stir in fresh chopped basil and season with salt and pepper to taste.

6. **Serve**:

    - Serve the pasta hot, garnished with additional basil leaves and a drizzle of extra virgin olive oil. Freshly grated Parmesan or pecorino cheese can be offered on the side, although traditionally, cheese is often omitted in seafood pasta in Italy.

Flavor Profile

Sardinian Seafood Pasta with Cherry Tomatoes and Basil offers a delightful combination of sweet and savory flavors enhanced by the freshness of the seafood and herbs. The cherry tomatoes provide a juicy, slightly acidic taste that complements the briny flavor of the seafood, while the basil adds a fresh, aromatic touch.

Serving Suggestions

This dish pairs beautifully with a chilled glass of Vermentino or another light, crisp white wine that complements the flavors of the seafood. A simple side salad dressed with lemon and olive oil makes a perfect accompaniment to this light yet satisfying meal.

Sardinian Seafood Pasta is a celebration of the Mediterranean lifestyle, where diet is linked closely with health and longevity, showcasing that delicious food and good health go hand in hand.

7.3 Greek Moussaka with Eggplant and Bechamel Sauce

Greek Moussaka is a traditional dish that epitomizes the rich culinary heritage of Greece, combining layers of flavor and texture into a comforting and luxurious meal. This version features layers of roasted eggplant, a spiced meat sauce, and is topped with a creamy béchamel sauce, making it a hearty dish that's perfect for family gatherings and special occasions.

Ingredients and Their Benefits

- **Eggplant**: The base layer of the dish, eggplant is a fiber-rich vegetable that's low in calories but high in nutrients, providing potassium, manganese, and antioxidants.

- **Ground Meat**: Typically made with lamb or beef, the meat layer adds protein and richness to the dish, making it filling and satisfying. The meat is seasoned with spices like cinnamon and nutmeg, which add a distinctive warm flavor.
- **Tomatoes**: Used in the meat sauce, tomatoes provide vitamin C, potassium, and lycopene, an antioxidant with heart health benefits.
- **Béchamel Sauce**: A creamy sauce made from milk, flour, and butter, topped with a bit of cheese. This layer adds a velvety texture and rich flavor, as well as calcium from the dairy ingredients.

Cooking Process

1. **Prepare the Eggplant**:
    - Slice the eggplants into rounds, salt them lightly, and set aside for about 30 minutes to draw out moisture. Pat dry, brush with olive oil, and roast in a preheated oven at 400°F (200°C) until soft and golden, about 20-30 minutes.
2. **Make the Meat Sauce**:
    - In a large skillet, brown the ground meat, breaking it up into small pieces. Add chopped onions and minced garlic, cooking until softened. Stir in grated

tomatoes, a dash of red wine, cinnamon, nutmeg, and season with salt and pepper. Simmer until the sauce thickens.

3. **Prepare the Béchamel Sauce**:
    - In a saucepan, melt butter over medium heat. Whisk in flour until smooth, then gradually add milk, stirring constantly until the sauce thickens. Season with nutmeg, salt, and pepper. Remove from heat and stir in a beaten egg for extra richness, ensuring the egg doesn't scramble.
4. **Assemble the Moussaka**:
    - In a baking dish, layer the roasted eggplant slices, followed by the meat sauce. Repeat the layers until all ingredients are used, finishing with a layer of eggplant. Pour the béchamel sauce over the top, spreading it evenly.
5. **Bake**:
    - Sprinkle the béchamel with grated Parmesan or kefalotyri cheese and bake in the oven at 350°F (175°C) for about 45 minutes, or until the top is bubbly and golden brown.
6. **Rest and Serve**:

- Let the moussaka sit for about 20 minutes after baking. This resting period helps the layers set, making it easier to cut and serve. Serve warm with a side of crusty bread or a simple salad.

Flavor Profile

Greek Moussaka with Eggplant and Bechamel Sauce offers a complex array of flavors and textures. The eggplant provides a soft, creamy base, contrasted by the savory, spiced meat sauce and the smooth, rich béchamel. The warming spices infuse the dish with a subtle sweetness that complements the savory components perfectly.

Serving Suggestions

Moussaka is a filling dish best enjoyed as the centerpiece of the meal. It pairs well with a light, acidic salad to cut through the richness, such as a Greek salad or a simple arugula salad with lemon vinaigrette. For wine pairings, a robust red wine like a Greek Agiorgitiko or a Cabernet Sauvignon can stand up to the richness of the dish.

This Greek Moussaka with Eggplant and Bechamel Sauce is more than just a meal; it's a celebration of Greek culinary traditions and a testament to the comforting power of well-prepared food. It's a dish meant for sharing, embodying the Mediterranean emphasis on meals as a focal point for family and social gatherings.

7.4 Sardinian Roasted Pork with Myrtle

Sardinian Roasted Pork with Myrtle is a celebration of the island's rich culinary traditions, marrying the robust flavors of pork with the aromatic essence of myrtle leaves. This dish reflects the deep connection between Sardinian cuisine and the native flora, using locally sourced ingredients that imbue the meat with distinctive flavors not commonly found elsewhere.

Ingredients and Their Benefits

- **Pork Loin**: A lean cut of meat that becomes tender and juicy when cooked properly. Pork is a good source of protein and provides essential vitamins and minerals.
- **Myrtle Leaves**: Used both fresh and dried, myrtle leaves are a staple in Sardinian cooking. They impart a subtle, slightly bitter flavor that complements the richness of the pork. Myrtle is also noted for its aromatic properties, which add a unique depth to the dish.
- **Garlic**: Adds a pungent kick that enhances the meat's natural flavors. Garlic is well-known for its health benefits, including its ability to

support cardiovascular health and its anti-inflammatory properties.

Cooking Process

1. **Prepare the Pork**:
   - Begin by trimming any excess fat from the pork loin and making shallow cuts across the top to help the seasoning penetrate more deeply.
2. **Marinate the Meat**:
   - Create a marinade by finely chopping fresh myrtle leaves and garlic, then mixing them with olive oil, salt, and pepper. Rub this mixture all over the pork loin, ensuring it gets into all the cuts and crevices. Let the pork marinate for several hours, or ideally overnight, in the refrigerator to enhance the flavor.
3. **Roast the Pork**:
   - Preheat your oven to 325°F (165°C). Place the marinated pork in a roasting pan and cover it lightly with foil to keep the moisture in. Roast the pork for about 1.5 to 2 hours, or until the meat is tender and fully cooked. For the last 30 minutes, remove the foil to allow the outside of the pork to brown and crisp up.

4. **Rest and Serve**:

    - Once cooked, let the pork rest for about 10-15 minutes before slicing. This allows the juices to redistribute throughout the meat, ensuring it is juicy and flavorful when served.

Flavor Profile

The Sardinian Roasted Pork with Myrtle features a harmonious blend of the rich, savory taste of pork with the unique, herbaceous notes of myrtle leaves. The garlic adds a bold flavor that is mellowed by the slow roasting process, resulting in a dish that is both refined and satisfying.

Serving Suggestions

Serve the roasted pork with a side of roasted vegetables, such as potatoes, carrots, and onions, which can be cooked in the same pan to absorb the meat's flavors. A simple salad dressed with olive oil and lemon can add a fresh, light contrast to the meal.

This Sardinian Roasted Pork with Myrtle not only offers a delectable taste experience but also embodies the essence of Sardinian cooking—simple ingredients brought to life with traditional herbs and techniques. It’s a perfect dish for special occasions or a family dinner, bringing a taste of Sardinian heritage to the table.

7.5 Ikarian Longevity Stew

Ikarian Longevity Stew is a nourishing dish deeply rooted in the dietary traditions of Ikaria, a Greek island renowned for the longevity of its residents. This stew is a testament to the local belief in the power of natural, simple foods to not only sustain life but enhance its quality and duration. Composed primarily of black-eyed peas, wild greens, and a generous amount of olive oil, this stew embodies the principles of the Mediterranean diet, which emphasizes legumes, vegetables, and healthy fats.

Ingredients and Their Benefits

- **Black-eyed Peas**: These legumes are a fantastic source of protein and fiber, essential for maintaining muscle strength and digestive health. They are also rich in key nutrients like potassium and zinc.
- **Wild Greens**: Typically includes dandelion, mustard greens, or whatever is seasonally available. These greens are packed with antioxidants, vitamins A, C, and K, and minerals such as iron and calcium, which support bone health and help combat inflammation.
- **Olive Oil**: A cornerstone of the Mediterranean diet, olive oil is high in monounsaturated fats and antioxidants, particularly oleocanthal,

which has anti-inflammatory properties similar to ibuprofen.

Cooking Process

1. **Prepare the Ingredients**:
   - Soak the black-eyed peas overnight to soften them, then drain and rinse. Gather fresh wild greens and wash them thoroughly to remove any dirt.
2. **Cook the Black-eyed Peas**:
   - In a large pot, add the black-eyed peas and cover with water. Bring to a boil, then reduce the heat and simmer until they are nearly tender, about 45 minutes to 1 hour.
3. **Add the Greens**:
   - Roughly chop the wild greens and add them to the pot with the peas. Continue to simmer, allowing the greens to wilt and meld with the legumes.
4. **Season the Stew**:
   - Generously drizzle olive oil over the stew—don't be shy, as the oil is integral to its flavor and health benefits. Season with salt, pepper, and a squeeze of lemon juice to enhance the flavors. For added depth,

some locals might add a pinch of smoked paprika or a bay leaf during cooking.

5. **Simmer to Perfection**:

    - Let the stew simmer on low heat for an additional 30 minutes, or until everything is tender and the flavors have combined beautifully. The result should be a rich, hearty stew with a slightly thickened broth.

Flavor Profile

Ikarian Longevity Stew offers a comforting, earthy flavor with the natural sweetness of the peas balancing the slight bitterness of the wild greens. The olive oil adds a smooth, rich dimension that ties all the ingredients together, while the lemon juice provides a bright finishing note.

Serving Suggestions

Serve the stew as a warm, filling meal with crusty whole-grain bread to soak up the delicious juices. It can be paired with a simple salad dressed with olive oil and vinegar for a complete, nutritionally balanced meal.

Ikarian Longevity Stew isn't just food; it's a reflection of a lifestyle that values slow cooking, natural ingredients, and eating practices that have supported the health and longevity of Ikarians for generations.

This dish is a celebration of life, tradition, and the joys of simple, wholesome food.

7.6 Sardinian Clam and Fennel Soup

Sardinian Clam and Fennel Soup is a delightful showcase of Sardinia's abundant seafood and its knack for pairing fresh catch with aromatic vegetables. This soup, with its simple yet elegant flavors, is a testament to the island's culinary traditions that emphasize freshness and regional ingredients.

Ingredients and Their Benefits

- **Clams**: These shellfish are not only delicious but also pack a hefty dose of lean protein, iron, and essential omega-3 fatty acids, which are vital for heart and brain health.
- **Fennel**: This bulbous vegetable lends a subtle aniseed flavor that complements seafood beautifully. Fennel is also rich in fiber, vitamin C, and potent antioxidants.
- **Tomatoes**: Add a touch of sweetness and acidity, while providing lycopene, vitamin C, and potassium, which are great for heart health.
- **White Wine**: A splash of white wine in cooking enhances flavor and adds a depth of complexity to the broth. The alcohol content evaporates

during cooking, leaving behind an aromatic base that elevates the other ingredients.

Cooking Process

1. **Prepare the Ingredients**:
    - Rinse the clams under cold running water, scrubbing their shells to remove any sand or grit. Chop the fennel bulb finely, dice the tomatoes, and mince a few cloves of garlic.
2. **Sauté the Vegetables**:
    - In a large pot, heat a drizzle of olive oil over medium heat. Add the chopped fennel and minced garlic, sautéing until the fennel becomes translucent and aromatic. Be careful not to let the garlic burn.
3. **Deglaze with Wine**:
    - Pour in a good splash of white wine, letting it simmer and reduce slightly, which releases all the delicious flavors stuck to the bottom of the pan.
4. **Add the Tomatoes and Broth**:
    - Stir in the diced tomatoes and cook until they begin to break down. Then add a fish

or vegetable broth to create the soup base. Bring the mixture to a gentle simmer.

5. **Cook the Clams**:
   - Add the clams to the pot, cover, and cook over medium heat. The clams are ready when they've opened up, which usually takes about 5 to 10 minutes. Discard any clams that do not open.
6. **Final Seasoning**:
   - Season the soup with salt and freshly ground black pepper to taste. Finish by stirring in a handful of chopped fresh parsley for color and freshness.

Flavor Profile

This soup is light yet brimming with flavor. The clams bring a briny depth, while the fennel provides a bright, almost licorice-like taste that's perfectly balanced by the acidity and sweetness of the tomatoes. The white wine rounds out the flavors with its fruity notes, making the broth rich and satisfying.

Serving Suggestions

Serve this soup hot, accompanied by crusty Sardinian bread or a slice of toasted baguette for dipping into the savory broth. It's perfect as a starter for a larger meal or as a light main course, paired with a crisp, dry white wine like Vermentino, which complements the seafood flavors beautifully.

Sardinian Clam and Fennel Soup not only warms the belly but also captures the essence of Sardinian cooking—fresh, simple, and sea-centered, reflecting the island's deep connection with its natural resources and culinary heritage.

7.7 Grilled Octopus over Ikarian Fava

Grilled Octopus over Ikarian Fava is a celebrated dish in Ikaria, known for its exceptional blend of sea and land flavors. This dish highlights the traditional Greek technique of pairing tender seafood with hearty legumes, creating a balanced, protein-rich meal that's as nutritious as it is delicious.

Ingredients and Their Benefits

- **Octopus**: A staple in Mediterranean cuisine, octopus is low in fat and high in protein, making it an excellent choice for a lean source of energy. It is also rich in omega-3 fatty acids, which are crucial for heart health and cognitive function.
- **Fava Beans**: These creamy legumes are not only a fantastic source of plant-based protein but also provide dietary fiber, potassium, and iron, supporting digestive health and energy levels.

- **Olive Oil**: Used in both the fava bean puree and to finish the octopus, olive oil adds a silky texture and heart-healthy fats to the dish.
- **Lemon and Herbs**: Fresh lemon juice and a mix of herbs like oregano and parsley brighten the dish, adding antioxidants and enhancing the flavors with their freshness.

Cooking Process

1. **Prepare the Octopus**:
    - Begin by cleaning the octopus, removing the beak and ink sac, and rinsing it under cold water. To tenderize the octopus, simmer it in a large pot of water with a cork (a traditional Greek method) for about 45-60 minutes until it is tender.
2. **Cook the Fava Beans**:
    - Rinse the dried fava beans and boil them until completely soft. Drain and while still warm, blend with olive oil, lemon juice, and a touch of garlic until smooth and creamy. Season with salt and pepper to taste.
3. **Grill the Octopus**:
    - Once the octopus is tender, marinate it briefly in olive oil, lemon juice, and chopped herbs. Then, grill it over high

heat for a few minutes on each side until the skin is crisp and slightly charred.

4. **Assemble the Dish**:
   - Spread a generous layer of the fava bean puree on a platter. Slice the grilled octopus and arrange it over the puree. Drizzle with more olive oil and lemon juice, and garnish with additional herbs.

Flavor Profile

This dish offers a delightful contrast of textures and flavors. The octopus provides a slight chewiness that is complemented by the smooth, rich texture of the fava bean puree. The char from the grill introduces a smoky flavor, which pairs beautifully with the bright, zesty notes of lemon and the earthiness of the herbs.

Serving Suggestions

Grilled Octopus over Ikarian Fava is best served immediately while the octopus is warm and the puree is creamy. It pairs wonderfully with a crisp white wine, such as an Assyrtiko, which can stand up to the robust flavors of the dish. For a complete meal, accompany it with a side of mixed greens dressed in a simple vinaigrette.

This dish not only captures the essence of Ikarian cuisine, with its focus on longevity and health, but also provides a culinary experience that is both grounding and uplifting, showcasing how simple ingredients from the earth and sea can be transformed into a sophisticated, flavorful meal.

7.8 Sardinian Culurgiones

Sardinian Culurgiones are a distinctive type of handmade pasta that encapsulates the rich culinary traditions of Sardinia. These elegantly shaped dumplings are stuffed with a flavorful mixture of potatoes, fresh mint, and Pecorino cheese, offering a delightful combination of textures and tastes that speak to the island's pastoral heritage.

Ingredients and Their Benefits

- **Potatoes**: The primary filling ingredient, potatoes provide a creamy texture and are a good source of vitamin C, potassium, and dietary fiber.
- **Mint**: Adds a refreshing, aromatic note to the filling, enhancing the flavors with its cool, bright taste.
- **Pecorino Cheese**: A sharp, salty cheese made from sheep's milk, Pecorino adds depth and richness to the filling, as well as calcium and protein.
- **Pasta Dough**: Typically made from a simple mix of flour and water, the dough is rolled thin and

then expertly shaped to encase the filling. The handmade process results in a tender, chewy texture that is a hallmark of artisanal pasta.

- **Tomato Sauce**: Fresh tomatoes cooked down into a sauce form the perfect accompaniment to the rich, savory flavors of the culurgiones, providing acidity and sweetness as well as lycopene, an antioxidant known for its health benefits.

Cooking Process

1. **Prepare the Filling**:
    - Boil the potatoes until tender, then mash them. Mix in finely chopped fresh mint and grated Pecorino cheese. Season with salt and pepper to taste.
2. **Make the Pasta Dough**:
    - Combine flour with water and a pinch of salt, knead into a smooth, elastic dough. Let it rest covered for about 30 minutes. Then, roll it out thinly on a floured surface.
3. **Shape the Culurgiones**:
    - Cut circles out of the dough using a cookie cutter or a glass. Place a spoonful of the potato mixture in the center of each circle. Fold the dough over the filling to form a

half-moon shape, then seal the edges by pinching and crimping them decoratively, which is characteristic of culurgiones.

4. **Cook the Pasta**:
    - Bring a large pot of salted water to a boil. Add the culurgiones and cook for about 4-5 minutes or until they float to the surface, indicating they are done.
5. **Prepare the Tomato Sauce**:
    - Simultaneously, in a separate pan, heat olive oil over medium heat. Add minced garlic and cook until fragrant. Pour in crushed tomatoes and simmer to let the flavors meld. Season with salt, pepper, and a sprinkle of sugar to balance the acidity.
6. **Serve**:
    - Drain the culurgiones and serve them hot, topped with the fresh tomato sauce. Garnish with extra grated Pecorino and a few mint leaves.

Flavor Profile

Culurgiones offer a delightful taste experience where the earthy sweetness of the potatoes complements the salty sharpness of the Pecorino and the fresh, cool undertones of mint. The simple tomato sauce enhances the dumplings with its bright, tangy flavor, making each bite perfectly balanced.

Serving Suggestions

Sardinian Culurgiones can be served as a main dish accompanied by a crisp green salad or as part of a larger Italian feast that might include antipasti and a second course of meat or fish. Pair with a medium-bodied Sardinian red wine, such as Cannonau, to elevate the dining experience.

This dish is not just a meal but an expression of Sardinian culture and artisanship, showcasing the importance of handmade techniques and local ingredients in creating food that is deeply satisfying and rich in heritage.

7.9 Ikarian Baked Sardines

Ikarian Baked Sardines are a quintessential dish from the island of Ikaria, renowned for its residents' longevity and healthful lifestyles. This recipe emphasizes the natural flavors of the Mediterranean with minimalistic preparation, highlighting the fresh, local seafood that is a staple in the Ikarian diet. Sardines, known for their rich omega-3 fatty acid content, are prepared with aromatic herbs and a crispy breadcrumb topping, making them not only nutritious but also delicious.

Ingredients and Their Benefits

- **Sardines**: These small fish are one of the most nutrient-rich seafood options, loaded with essential omega-3 fatty acids, which are crucial for cardiovascular health, brain function, and reducing inflammation.
- **Herbs**: Typically, a combination of parsley, oregano, and garlic is used to season the fish, providing antioxidant benefits and enhancing the dish with fresh, vibrant flavors.
- **Breadcrumbs**: Add a satisfying crunch to the dish, improving the texture contrast while also helping to retain the moisture of the fish during baking.
- **Olive Oil**: Drizzled over the sardines, olive oil helps crisp up the breadcrumbs and adds healthy fats to the dish, further enriching its heart-healthy profile.

Cooking Process

1. **Prepare the Sardines**:
    - Clean the sardines by removing the scales, guts, and spines. Rinse them under cold water and pat them dry. This preparation ensures that the fish cooks evenly and integrates well with the flavors of the herbs and oil.
2. **Season the Fish**:

- In a bowl, mix finely chopped parsley, oregano, minced garlic, salt, and pepper. Rub this herb mixture inside and outside of the sardines to infuse them with these aromatic flavors.

3. **Breadcrumb Topping**:

   - In a separate bowl, combine breadcrumbs with a little olive oil and additional chopped herbs. This mixture should be crumbly yet slightly moist, ready to adhere to the fish.

4. **Assemble and Bake**:

   - Preheat the oven to 375°F (190°C). Arrange the sardines in a single layer in a baking dish. Sprinkle the breadcrumb mixture over the sardines, ensuring they are evenly coated. Drizzle generously with olive oil, which will help crisp the topping and add richness.
   - Bake in the preheated oven for about 15-20 minutes, or until the breadcrumbs are golden and the sardines are cooked through.

5. **Serving**:

   - Serve the sardines hot, straight from the oven. They can be accompanied by a slice of lemon for an added zesty flavor and a fresh green salad or a side of roasted vegetables.

Flavor Profile

The Ikarian Baked Sardines offer a delightful combination of the ocean's freshness with the earthy, aromatic qualities of the herbs. The olive oil and breadcrumbs create a textural contrast that makes each bite satisfying and complex.

Serving Suggestions

This dish is perfect as a light dinner or a substantial appetizer. It embodies the principles of the Mediterranean diet, focusing on simplicity, freshness, and the nutritional synergy of combining plant-based ingredients with healthy seafood. Pair this dish with a crisp white wine, such as a Greek Assyrtiko, to complement the flavors and elevate the dining experience.

Ikarian Baked Sardines not only provide a taste of the Mediterranean but also offer a heart-healthy meal that aligns with the dietary habits that contribute to the remarkable longevity of Ikaria's residents.

7.10 Sardinian Lamb with Artichokes

Sardinian Lamb with Artichokes is a traditional dish that encapsulates the rustic and robust flavors of

Sardinia. This slow-cooked stew marries tender lamb with the earthy tones of artichokes and the briny kick of olives, all infused with the aromatic herbs typical of the island. It's a hearty, comforting dish that exemplifies the Sardinian approach to combining meats and vegetables for a balanced, flavorful meal.

Ingredients and Their Benefits

- **Lamb**: Rich in high-quality protein and essential vitamins and minerals, including iron, zinc, and vitamin B12. Lamb is particularly valued in Sardinia for its depth of flavor and nutritional value.
- **Artichokes**: Known for their fiber content and distinctive taste, artichokes add texture and a host of beneficial antioxidants to the dish.
- **Olives**: Add a touch of Mediterranean zest, olives are rich in heart-healthy monounsaturated fats and contribute to the overall savory profile of the stew.
- **Sardinian Herbs**: Typically includes wild fennel, rosemary, and sage, which not only season the dish but also offer anti-inflammatory and digestive benefits.

Cooking Process

1. **Prepare the Lamb**:

- Begin by cutting the lamb into large chunks, seasoning with salt and freshly ground black pepper. Brown the lamb pieces in a heavy pot with a bit of olive oil to enhance their flavor and seal in the juices.

2. **Add the Aromatics and Vegetables**:

   - To the pot, add chopped onions and garlic, cooking until they are soft and translucent. Introduce the artichokes, which can be fresh or frozen, depending on availability.

3. **Build the Stew Base**:

   - Incorporate a handful of pitted olives, giving the dish its characteristic Mediterranean flavor. Add chopped tomatoes or a spoonful of tomato paste for richness and color.

4. **Season with Herbs**:

   - Stir in a generous amount of chopped Sardinian herbs such as fennel, rosemary, and sage. These herbs complement the strong flavors of the lamb and add a fresh, aromatic depth to the stew.

5. **Slow Cook**:

- Pour in enough water or broth to just cover the ingredients. Bring to a boil, then reduce the heat and let simmer, covered, for at least two hours. The long cooking time allows the lamb to become exceptionally tender and the flavors to meld beautifully.

6. **Final Adjustments**:
   - Once the lamb is tender and the artichokes are cooked through, adjust the seasoning with additional salt and pepper if needed. The stew should have a rich, cohesive flavor with a slightly thickened sauce.

Flavor Profile

Sardinian Lamb with Artichokes offers a complex taste experience where the rich, gamey flavor of the lamb contrasts with the subtle, slightly sweet and nutty flavor of the artichokes. The olives contribute a saline sharpness that cuts through the richness, while the herbs provide a fresh, aromatic lift.

Serving Suggestions

Serve this stew with a side of Sardinian flatbread or over a simple bed of polenta or couscous to soak up the delicious juices. Pair with a robust Sardinian red wine, such as Cannonau, which complements the rich flavors of the lamb.

This dish not only fills the kitchen with enticing aromas but also provides a comforting, satisfying meal that is perfect for gatherings with family and friends, reflecting the Sardinian culture's emphasis on communal dining and enjoying life's pleasures through good food.

These dishes not only offer a taste of Mediterranean life but also embody the dietary principles found in these regions, known for their contributions to health and longevity. Each recipe uses fresh, local ingredients that are minimally processed to preserve their nutritional integrity and enhance their natural flavors.

Chapter 8:

Snacks and Sweets Inspired by the Mediterranean Blue Zones

In the heart of the Mediterranean Blue Zones, snacks and sweets are not just treats but integral parts of a diet that balances indulgence with health. This chapter delves into the delicious, nutrient-rich snacks and desserts that are staples in the lives of some of the world's oldest and healthiest populations. From the sweet drizzles of honey on a Greek Baklava to the savory crunch of Sardinian Pistachio Biscotti, these recipes offer a taste of the Mediterranean's joyful and health-sustaining food culture. Each dish is crafted to not only satisfy the palate but also to nourish the body and soul, embodying the essence of Mediterranean hospitality and leisure. Join us as we explore how these delightful snacks and sweets contribute to longevity, ensuring each bite is as beneficial as it is delicious.

8.1 Ikarian Hummus with Roasted Red Pepper and Chickpeas

Ikarian Hummus with Roasted Red Pepper and Chickpeas is a vibrant and healthful dish that embodies the simplicity and nutritive richness of Ikarian cuisine. This twist on traditional hummus incorporates the sweet, smoky flavor of roasted red peppers, making it not only a delightful dip but also a nutritious snack that can be enjoyed at any time of the day.

Ingredients and Their Benefits

- **Chickpeas**: The base of this hummus, chickpeas are a fantastic source of plant-based protein, fiber, and essential nutrients like iron and phosphorus, which support energy levels and bone health.
- **Roasted Red Peppers**: Add a sweet, smoky depth to the hummus. They are also high in vitamins A and C, which are important for immune health and skin integrity.
- **Tahini**: Made from ground sesame seeds, tahini is rich in healthy fats, calcium, and has a creamy texture that enhances the body of the hummus.
- **Olive Oil**: A staple in Ikarian cooking, olive oil is used for its heart-healthy fats and its ability to carry flavors throughout the dish.

- **Lemon Juice**: Adds a bright, tangy note to the hummus, lifting the flavors and adding a dose of vitamin C.
- **Garlic**: Provides a pungent kick that complements the sweetness of the peppers and deepens the overall flavor profile of the hummus.
- **Spices**: A touch of cumin and smoked paprika not only enhances the taste but also adds a layer of anti-inflammatory benefits.

Cooking Process

1. **Prepare the Roasted Red Peppers**:
    - If using fresh red peppers, char them over an open flame or roast in the oven until the skin blisters. Once cooled, peel off the skin, remove the seeds, and slice the flesh into strips.
2. **Blend the Ingredients**:
    - In a food processor, combine cooked or canned chickpeas (drained and rinsed), roasted red pepper strips, tahini, minced garlic, lemon juice, olive oil, and spices. Blend until smooth. If the mixture is too thick, add a little water or additional lemon juice to reach the desired consistency.

3. **Season to Taste**:
    - Taste the hummus and adjust the seasoning with salt, more lemon juice, or spices as needed. The goal is to have a well-balanced mix of smoky, tangy, and savory flavors.
4. **Serve**:
    - Transfer the hummus to a serving bowl. Drizzle with a little more olive oil and perhaps a sprinkle of smoked paprika or chopped parsley for color.

Flavor Profile

This Ikarian Hummus is creamy, with a rich flavor profile that balances the earthiness of chickpeas with the sweet and smoky notes of roasted red peppers. The tahini adds a slight bitterness and nuttiness, while the lemon juice and spices provide a refreshing contrast that enhances the dish's complexity.

Serving Suggestions

Serve the hummus as a dip with an assortment of raw vegetables, whole-grain pita bread, or as a spread on sandwiches. It's perfect for a quick snack, a part of a mezze platter, or even as a light meal, providing sustained energy thanks to its high protein and fiber content.

This hummus not only offers a taste of Ikarian culinary traditions but also integrates the healthful principles of the Mediterranean diet, making it a perfect example of how diet can play a role in longevity and wellness.

8.2 Sardinian Olive Oil Cake with Orange Zest and Almonds

Sardinian Olive Oil Cake with Orange Zest and Almonds is a delightful dessert that highlights the rich culinary traditions of Sardinia. This cake uses olive oil as a key ingredient, replacing butter to create a moist texture and subtly rich flavor. Infused with the zest of fresh oranges and the crunch of almonds, this cake not only tantalizes the taste buds but also reflects the healthy, natural ingredients prevalent in Mediterranean cuisine.

Ingredients and Their Benefits

- **Olive Oil**: The star of this cake, olive oil provides a moist crumb and subtle fruitiness, while also contributing heart-healthy monounsaturated fats.
- **Orange Zest**: Adds a bright citrus flavor that pairs beautifully with the olive oil, while also providing vitamin C and bioflavonoids.

- **Almonds**: Offer a delightful crunch and are a good source of protein, healthy fats, and vitamin E, which is great for skin health.
- **Eggs**: Contribute to the structure and richness of the cake, adding high-quality protein.
- **Whole Wheat Flour**: Used instead of all-purpose flour to add fiber and nutrients, supporting a more nutritious profile.
- **Sugar**: While used in moderation, sugar helps create the sweet taste characteristic of cakes.

Cooking Process

1. **Prepare the Cake Batter**:
    - In a large mixing bowl, whisk together eggs and sugar until the mixture is pale and fluffy. Gradually whisk in the olive oil and continue to mix until well incorporated.
    - Stir in the orange zest to infuse the batter with citrus flavor.
    - In a separate bowl, mix whole wheat flour with a pinch of salt and baking powder. Gradually add the dry ingredients to the wet, mixing until just combined to keep the cake tender.

- Fold in roughly chopped almonds for added texture and nutty flavor.

2. **Bake the Cake**:
    - Pour the batter into a greased and floured cake pan—either a round pan for a traditional look or a loaf pan for a more casual presentation.
    - Bake in a preheated oven at 350°F (175°C) for about 30-40 minutes, or until a toothpick inserted in the center comes out clean. The top should be golden and spring back when touched.
3. **Cool and Serve**:
    - Let the cake cool in the pan for about 10 minutes, then turn out onto a wire rack to cool completely.
    - Once cooled, dust lightly with powdered sugar or drizzle with a simple glaze made from orange juice and powdered sugar for added sweetness and a glossy finish.

Flavor Profile

This Olive Oil Cake is wonderfully moist and fragrant, with the olive oil providing a unique flavor that is not overly assertive but pleasantly noticeable. The orange zest offers a fresh citrus note that complements the richness of the almonds and olive oil. The almonds not only add texture but also enhance the cake's flavor profile with their earthy taste.

Serving Suggestions

This cake is perfect as an afternoon treat with a cup of coffee or tea, or as a dessert served at the end of a meal. It pairs particularly well with a dollop of whipped cream or a scoop of vanilla ice cream, and a few fresh orange slices on the side to reinforce the citrus theme.

The Sardinian Olive Oil Cake with Orange Zest and Almonds showcases how traditional ingredients can be transformed into a delicious, modern dessert that remains true to the healthful principles of the Mediterranean diet, making it suitable for both everyday indulgence and special occasions.

8.3 Greek Baklava with Honey and Pistachios

Greek Baklava with Honey and Pistachios is a classic Mediterranean dessert known for its rich flavors and exquisite layers of texture. This traditional Greek pastry is made by layering thin sheets of phyllo dough with a generous amount of chopped pistachios, all soaked in a sweet honey syrup. It's a celebration of sweetness and nuttiness, showcasing the luxurious side of Mediterranean sweets.

Ingredients and Their Benefits

- **Phyllo Dough**: Provides the crispy, flaky layers that are iconic to baklava, offering a light texture that contrasts with the rich filling.
- **Pistachios**: These nuts are not only flavorful but also packed with nutrients, including healthy fats, protein, and fiber. They add a delightful crunch and vibrant color to the dessert.
- **Honey**: Acts as a natural sweetener and binds the layers of phyllo and pistachios together. Honey also offers antioxidants and can provide soothing effects to the digestive system.
- **Butter**: Used to brush between the layers of phyllo, butter helps achieve the golden, crispy texture while enhancing the flavor.
- **Cinnamon and Clove**: Spices that are often added to the nut mixture or syrup, providing warmth and depth to the flavor profile.

Cooking Process

1. **Prepare the Nut Mixture**:
    - Finely chop or grind the pistachios and mix them with cinnamon and a small amount of clove for added spice. This mixture will be layered between the phyllo sheets to create the rich, flavorful interior of the baklava.
2. **Assemble the Baklava**:

- Begin by buttering a baking dish. Lay down a sheet of phyllo dough, brush it with melted butter, and then place another sheet on top. Repeat this process until you have built up about 8 layers.
- Spread a layer of the pistachio mixture over the top phyllo layer, then continue layering more phyllo sheets and butter, followed by more nuts. Repeat this layering process, finishing with about 6-8 layers of phyllo on top.

3. **Cut and Bake**:
   - Preheat the oven to 350°F (175°C). Before baking, use a sharp knife to cut the baklava into diagonal or square pieces, allowing the syrup to soak into the pastry later.
   - Bake in the preheated oven for about 45-50 minutes, or until the phyllo is puffed and golden brown.
4. **Prepare the Honey Syrup**:
   - While the baklava bakes, prepare the syrup by boiling honey, water, a slice of lemon, and a stick of cinnamon to infuse flavor. Let it simmer until it thickens slightly.

5. **Finish with Syrup**:
    - As soon as the baklava comes out of the oven, pour the hot syrup over the hot pastry. This allows the syrup to seep into the layers, making the baklava moist and sweet.

Flavor Profile

Greek Baklava with Honey and Pistachios is intensely sweet with a profound nutty essence thanks to the pistachios. The spices, honey, and butter meld together to create a decadently sweet, aromatic, and rich dessert. The texture is a delightful contrast between the crispy phyllo and the soft, chewy filling.

Serving Suggestions

Baklava is best served at room temperature, often with a cup of strong coffee or tea to balance its sweetness. It's perfect for special occasions and celebrations, embodying the generous and indulgent spirit of Mediterranean hospitality.

This dessert not only delights the palate but also connects those who share it to centuries of Mediterranean culinary tradition, celebrating the region's penchant for combining simple ingredients to create extraordinary flavors.

8.4 Sardinian Pistachio Biscotti

Sardinian Pistachio Biscotti are delightful twice-baked cookies that combine the crunchiness of pistachios with the sweet, rustic charm of traditional Italian biscotti. These cookies are not only perfect for dipping in a cup of rich Italian espresso or a sweet glass of Vin Santo but also embody the essence of Sardinian baking, where simplicity meets exquisite flavors.

Ingredients and Their Benefits

- **Pistachios**: Known for their distinctive green color and sweet flavor, pistachios add texture and are a great source of healthy fats, protein, and fiber.
- **Flour**: Typically, all-purpose flour is used for its ability to create the perfect crumbly yet dense biscotti texture.
- **Sugar**: Adds sweetness and contributes to the golden-brown color when baked.
- **Eggs**: Bind the ingredients together and help in creating a firm texture that holds up well to dipping.
- **Vanilla Extract**: Adds a sweet, aromatic flavor that complements the pistachios beautifully.

- **Lemon Zest**: A hint of lemon zest can be added for a refreshing citrus note that cuts through the richness of the nuts.

Cooking Process

1. **Prepare the Dough**:
    - In a mixing bowl, combine sugar and eggs and beat until the mixture is light and fluffy. Stir in vanilla extract and lemon zest for added flavor.
    - Gradually mix in the flour and a pinch of salt until a sticky dough forms. Fold in chopped pistachios, distributing them evenly throughout the dough.
2. **Shape and First Bake**:
    - Preheat the oven to 350°F (175°C).
    - Turn the dough out onto a lightly floured surface and divide it into two equal parts. Shape each part into a log approximately 12 inches long and place on a baking sheet lined with parchment paper.
    - Flatten the logs slightly and bake for about 25-30 minutes, or until they are light golden brown.
3. **Second Bake**:

- Remove the logs from the oven and let them cool for a few minutes. Once they are cool enough to handle, cut each log diagonally into 1/2-inch thick slices using a sharp serrated knife.
- Arrange the slices cut side down on the baking sheet and return them to the oven. Bake for an additional 5-7 minutes on each side, or until they are crisp and golden.

Flavor Profile

Sardinian Pistachio Biscotti have a crunchy exterior with a slightly softer center. The pistachios provide a nutty flavor and a satisfying crunch, which contrasts nicely with the subtle sweetness of the biscotti dough. The addition of lemon zest offers a light, refreshing zing that makes these biscotti uniquely flavorful.

Serving Suggestions

Serve these biscotti as an accompaniment to coffee or dessert wine. They are ideal for a morning treat or as an after-dinner dessert that isn't overly sweet. The robust texture of biscotti makes them perfect for dipping, holding up well when submerged in a beverage.

Sardinian Pistachio Biscotti not only offer a delightful snack or dessert option but also embrace the Mediterranean tradition of using natural, wholesome ingredients to create treats that are both satisfying and conducive to a healthy lifestyle.

8.5 Ikarian Fig and Walnut Tart

The Ikarian Fig and Walnut Tart is a celebration of natural sweetness and rustic textures, encapsulating the essence of Ikaria's wholesome approach to desserts. This tart combines nutritious dried figs and hearty walnuts in a whole grain pastry shell, all sweetened with honey, aligning perfectly with the healthful eating habits that contribute to the longevity of Ikaria's residents.

Ingredients and Their Benefits

- **Dried Figs**: Rich in dietary fiber, potassium, and natural sugars, figs are excellent for digestive health and provide sustained energy.
- **Walnuts**: Loaded with omega-3 fatty acids, walnuts contribute to brain health and add a satisfying crunch.
- **Whole Grain Flour**: Used for the pastry shell, it offers more nutrients and fiber than refined flours, supporting heart health and digestion.
- **Honey**: A natural sweetener that provides antioxidants and a subtle sweetness without the spike in blood sugar levels associated with refined sugars.

- **Cinnamon**: Adds warmth and spice, complementing the sweet figs and earthy walnuts perfectly.

Cooking Process

1. **Prepare the Pastry Shell**:
    - In a large mixing bowl, combine whole grain flour, a pinch of salt, and cold butter cut into small cubes. Use your fingertips to rub the butter into the flour until the mixture resembles coarse breadcrumbs.
    - Gradually add cold water, stirring until the dough just comes together. Form the dough into a disk, wrap in cling film, and chill in the refrigerator for at least 30 minutes.
2. **Make the Filling**:
    - In a bowl, mix chopped dried figs and walnuts with a drizzle of honey and a sprinkle of cinnamon. Toss to coat evenly, ensuring that the figs and walnuts are well-marinated in the honey and spices.
3. **Assemble and Bake the Tart**:
    - Roll out the chilled dough on a lightly floured surface into a circle about 1/8 inch thick. Carefully transfer it to a tart

pan, pressing it into the corners and trimming the edges.

- Spread the fig and walnut mixture evenly over the pastry base.
- Bake in a preheated oven at 375°F (190°C) for about 25-30 minutes or until the pastry is golden and the filling is bubbly and caramelized.

Flavor Profile

The Ikarian Fig and Walnut Tart offers a delightful array of textures and flavors. The dried figs provide a chewy sweetness that contrasts beautifully with the crunchy walnuts. The whole grain crust adds a nutty flavor and a hearty bite, while the honey and cinnamon infuse the tart with warm, comforting notes.

Serving Suggestions

Serve this tart warm or at room temperature, perhaps accompanied by a scoop of Greek yogurt or a drizzle of extra honey. It pairs wonderfully with a cup of herbal tea or a strong coffee, making it an ideal dessert for any season.

This tart is not just a treat for the palate but also a heart-healthy option suitable for a lifestyle focused on longevity and wellness, reflecting the dietary traditions of Ikaria, where natural ingredients and simple preparations lead to delicious and healthful eating.

8.6 Sardinian Honey and Almond Nougat (Torrone)

Sardinian Honey and Almond Nougat, known locally as Torrone, is a cherished confection that epitomizes the artisanal and natural sweet-making traditions of Sardinia. This classic treat combines honey, whipped egg whites, and toasted almonds to create a nougat that is both delightfully chewy and richly flavored, symbolizing the simplicity and purity of the ingredients used in Sardinian cuisine.

Ingredients and Their Benefits

- **Honey**: Acts as a natural sweetener and binding agent. Honey is rich in antioxidants and provides a smooth, sticky consistency that is characteristic of good nougat.
- **Egg Whites**: When whipped, egg whites give the nougat its light, airy texture. They also serve as a protein source, making the nougat surprisingly filling.
- **Almonds**: Almonds are a staple in Mediterranean diets, known for their healthy fats, protein, and fiber. In nougat, they add a crunchy texture and nutty flavor, enhancing the overall taste and providing substantial nutritional benefits.

Cooking Process

1. **Prepare the Ingredients**:
   - Toast the almonds in a dry skillet until they are golden brown and fragrant. This enhances their flavor and adds an extra crunch to the nougat.
   - Line a baking dish with parchment paper and brush it lightly with oil to prevent the nougat from sticking.
2. **Make the Nougat Base**:
   - In a saucepan, combine honey and a splash of water. Heat over a medium flame, stirring constantly, until the honey becomes syrupy and reaches the hard crack stage (about 150°C or 302°F on a candy thermometer).
   - While the honey is heating, whip the egg whites to stiff peaks in a large, clean bowl.
3. **Combine and Set**:
   - Once the honey reaches the desired temperature, gradually pour it over the whipped egg whites while continuously beating. This will incorporate the honey into the egg whites without deflating them.

- Quickly fold in the toasted almonds, ensuring they are evenly distributed throughout the mixture.
- Pour the nougat mixture into the prepared dish, smoothing the top with a spatula. Allow it to set at room temperature until it is firm to the touch.

4. **Cut and Serve**:
    - Once set, lift the nougat out of the dish using the parchment paper and place it on a cutting board. Using a sharp knife, cut the nougat into bars or squares.
    - Store the nougat pieces in an airtight container to keep them chewy and fresh.

Flavor Profile

Sardinian Honey and Almond Nougat offers a perfect balance between the sweetness of honey and the nuttiness of toasted almonds. The texture is uniquely satisfying, with a firm yet chewy bite that melts in your mouth, punctuated by the crunch of almonds.

Serving Suggestions

Torrone is often enjoyed as a festive treat during holidays and special occasions. It pairs wonderfully with a cup of espresso or a glass of Sardinian dessert wine, such as Mirto, which complements its sweetness and rich flavors. It's also a popular gift item, representing the warmth and generosity of Sardinian hospitality.

This traditional nougat not only delights those who taste it but also carries with it the history and culinary heritage of Sardinia, making it a beloved treat that transcends generations.

8.7 Ikarian Petimezi Cookies

Ikarian Petimezi Cookies are a wholesome and flavorful treat, embodying the health-conscious and natural ingredient-focused culinary traditions of Ikaria, Greece. Made with grape molasses (petimezi), olive oil, and whole wheat flour, these cookies offer a rustic, nutritious snack that not only satisfies the sweet tooth but also provides a substantial energy boost.

Ingredients and Their Benefits

- **Grape Molasses (Petimezi)**: A natural sweetener made from condensed grape must, petimezi is rich in iron and antioxidants. It imparts a deep, fruity sweetness to the cookies without any refined sugars.
- **Olive Oil**: Used instead of butter, olive oil adds a subtle fruity flavor and contributes healthy monounsaturated fats, which are heart-healthy and provide a moist texture to the cookies.

- **Whole Wheat Flour**: Offers a higher nutritional content than refined flours, including more fiber, which aids in digestion and provides a slower release of energy.
- **Cinnamon**: Adds a warm spice that complements the sweetness of the molasses, and it has anti-inflammatory properties.
- **Sesame Seeds**: Provide a nutty taste and a crunch, and are a good source of calcium and healthy fats.

Cooking Process

1. **Prepare the Dough**:
    - In a large mixing bowl, combine whole wheat flour, a pinch of salt, and cinnamon. Mix well to distribute the spices evenly.
    - In another bowl, whisk together grape molasses and olive oil until fully combined.
    - Gradually add the wet ingredients to the dry ingredients, stirring until a cohesive dough forms. If the dough is too sticky, add a little more flour until it's manageable.
2. **Add Sesame Seeds**:

- Pour sesame seeds into a small dish. Scoop small portions of the cookie dough and roll them into balls. Press each ball into the sesame seeds, coating one side.

3. **Bake the Cookies**:

    - Preheat your oven to 350°F (175°C). Line a baking sheet with parchment paper.
    - Place the cookie dough balls on the prepared baking sheet, sesame seed side up, pressing them slightly to flatten.
    - Bake in the preheated oven for 10-12 minutes or until the edges are just turning golden. The cookies should be soft but will firm up as they cool.

Flavor Profile

Ikarian Petimezi Cookies are distinctly sweet with a rich, earthy undertone from the grape molasses, balanced by the spicy hint of cinnamon. The olive oil provides a slight savory note that complements the sweet molasses, while the sesame seeds add a satisfying crunch and nutty flavor.

Serving Suggestions

These cookies are perfect as a morning snack with coffee or tea, offering a substantial energy boost to start the day. They can also be enjoyed as an afternoon pick-me-up, ideally paired with a small cup of Greek coffee or herbal tea. Their robust flavor and nutritious profile make them suitable for those looking for a healthier cookie option that doesn't sacrifice taste for wellness.

The Ikarian Petimezi Cookies not only provide a delicious treat but also reflect the longevity practices of Ikaria, where natural ingredients and wholesome foods play a central role in the diet.

8.8 Sardinian Seadas

Sardinian Seadas, or Sebadas, are a traditional dessert from Sardinia that perfectly encapsulates the island's culinary ethos of simple ingredients executed with precision. These pastries combine the savory tang of fresh pecorino cheese with the bright zestiness of lemon, all encased in a crisp, fried pastry shell. Drizzled with rich, floral honey upon serving, Seadas offer a delightful contrast of flavors and textures that are both surprising and satisfying.

Ingredients and Their Benefits

- **Pecorino Cheese**: This sharp, salty cheese made from sheep’s milk is a staple in Sardinian cuisine. It adds depth and a complex flavor profile to the Seadas.
- **Lemon Zest**: Provides a fresh, citrusy brightness that cuts through the richness of the cheese and pastry, enhancing the overall flavor of the dish.

- **Pastry Dough**: Typically made from flour, water, and lard or butter, the dough is rolled thin and then fried to achieve a golden, flaky texture.
- **Honey**: A drizzle of local Sardinian honey not only adds a touch of sweetness but also brings its own antioxidants and soothing qualities, creating a perfect balance to the savory filling.

Cooking Process

1. **Prepare the Dough and Filling**:
    - To make the dough, mix flour with a pinch of salt and add small pieces of cold butter or lard. Gradually add cold water to form a smooth and elastic dough. Let it rest for about 30 minutes.
    - For the filling, grate fresh pecorino cheese and mix it with lemon zest to infuse it with citrus flavor.
2. **Assemble the Seadas**:
    - Divide the rested dough into small balls. Roll out each ball into a thin circle.
    - Place a generous amount of the pecorino and lemon zest mixture in the center of half of the dough circles.
    - Cover each filled circle with another circle of dough. Seal the edges by pressing them with a fork, ensuring the cheese is completely encased.

3. **Fry the Seadas**:
    - Heat a deep layer of vegetable oil in a frying pan until it reaches a medium-high temperature.
    - Carefully place the Seadas in the hot oil, frying them until they are golden brown on both sides. This should take about 2-3 minutes per side.

4. **Serve with Honey**:
    - Drain the fried Seadas on paper towels to remove excess oil.
    - While still warm, drizzle them generously with honey. The heat of the Seadas will slightly melt the honey, allowing it to seep into the pastry.

Flavor Profile

Sardinian Seadas offer a remarkable taste experience where the salty sharpness of the pecorino cheese meets the sweet floral notes of the honey, all encased in a crisp, buttery pastry. The addition of lemon zest adds a refreshing layer that lifts the flavors, making each bite complex and memorable.

Serving Suggestions

Seadas are traditionally served warm as a dessert after a meal, often accompanied by a glass of Mirto, a

Sardinian myrtle berry liqueur, or a cup of strong Italian coffee. They can also be presented as part of a larger dessert spread, offering guests a taste of Sardinian tradition that is both rich in flavor and history.
This dish not only delights the palate but also tells the story of Sardinia's pastoral traditions and its people's mastery in turning simple, locally sourced ingredients into extraordinary culinary creations.

8.9 Ikarian Herbal Tea Infusion

The Ikarian Herbal Tea Infusion epitomizes the essence of Ikaria's pristine natural environment, a key factor contributing to the island's recognition as a Blue Zone where inhabitants enjoy remarkable longevity. This tea is crafted from a blend of wild herbs including sage, thyme, and rosemary, each collected from the rugged hillsides of Ikaria. These herbs are not only cherished for their aromatic qualities but also for their potent health benefits, particularly their strong antioxidant properties.

Ingredients and Their Benefits

- **Sage**: This herb is revered for its anti-inflammatory, antioxidant, and antimicrobial properties. Sage tea is traditionally consumed in Ikaria for its potential to enhance brain function and memory, as well as for its calming effects, which can alleviate throat irritation and promote digestive health.

- **Thyme**: Rich in vitamins C and A, thyme supports the immune system. It's also a powerful antibacterial and antifungal agent, making it effective in combating respiratory infections—a common use in traditional Ikarian households.
- **Rosemary**: Known for its ability to improve concentration and boost memory, rosemary is also celebrated for its role in enhancing circulatory health and providing anti-inflammatory benefits.

Brewing Process

1. **Harvest and Prepare the Herbs**:
    - Ideally, fresh herbs are harvested early in the morning for peak potency. Clean the herbs gently to remove any dirt while preserving their delicate oils.
    - If fresh herbs are unavailable, dried versions can be used. These should be stored in a cool, dark place to maintain their medicinal qualities.
2. **Steeping the Tea**:
    - For one cup of tea, use about one teaspoon of dried herbs or one tablespoon

of fresh herbs. Adjust according to taste preference for stronger or more subtle flavors.

- Boil water and pour it over the herbs in a teapot or directly in a cup. Cover the vessel to prevent the escape of aromatic oils.
- Let the herbs steep for 5 to 10 minutes, depending on desired strength. The longer the steep, the more potent the infusion.

3. **Straining and Serving**:
    - Strain the tea to remove the herb leaves. Serve the infusion warm.
    - Optionally, sweeten with honey, which complements the herbal flavors and adds its own antibacterial properties, or add a slice of lemon for a vitamin C boost and enhanced flavor.

Flavor Profile

The Ikarian Herbal Tea Infusion offers a complex flavor profile characterized by the earthy and somewhat peppery notes of sage, the slightly sweet and pungent taste of thyme, and the woody, citrus-like flavor of rosemary. Together, these herbs create a soothing and aromatic beverage that invigorates the senses.

Serving Suggestions

This herbal tea is perfect for morning or evening enjoyment. In Ikaria, it's often consumed in the late afternoon as a relaxing beverage to wind down the day. It's also served to guests as a sign of hospitality and shared during community gatherings, reinforcing social bonds—a key aspect of the Ikarian lifestyle.

The Ikarian Herbal Tea Infusion is more than just a beverage; it's a daily ritual that supports long life and well-being, embodying the holistic approach to health that is central to the Blue Zone way of living.

8.10 Sardinian Ricotta and Lemon Cake

The Sardinian Ricotta and Lemon Cake is a delightful dessert that showcases the rich culinary traditions of Sardinia, combining local dairy products with the bright, refreshing flavors of citrus. This cake is known for its incredibly moist texture and light, fluffy consistency, making it a favored treat for both casual and festive occasions.

Ingredients and Their Benefits

- **Ricotta Cheese**: Fresh ricotta is the star ingredient of this cake, providing a creamy texture and a slightly sweet, milky flavor. Ricotta is rich in protein and calcium, making it a healthier alternative to more processed fats used in traditional cakes.

- **Lemons**: The zest and juice of lemons not only add a vibrant, tangy flavor but also contribute vitamin C and other beneficial antioxidants that help boost immune health.
- **Eggs**: Provide structure and lift to the cake, contributing to its light, airy texture while also offering protein and essential nutrients.
- **Sugar**: Adds sweetness and helps in the caramelization and browning of the crust.
- **Flour**: Forms the foundation of the cake, giving it body and texture. Using a mixture of all-purpose and a little almond flour can enhance the flavor and keep the cake tender.
- **Baking Powder**: Acts as a leavening agent, ensuring the cake rises properly during baking.

Cooking Process

1. **Prepare the Batter**:
    - In a large mixing bowl, whisk the ricotta cheese until smooth. Add sugar and lemon zest, mixing until well combined. Beat in eggs one at a time, ensuring each is fully incorporated before adding the next.

- In a separate bowl, combine the flour, baking powder, and a pinch of salt. Gradually sift and fold the dry ingredients into the wet mixture, alternating with lemon juice to maintain a smooth consistency without overmixing.

2. **Bake the Cake**:

   - Preheat your oven to 350°F (175°C). Grease a round cake pan and line it with parchment paper for easy removal.
   - Pour the batter into the prepared pan, smoothing the top with a spatula.
   - Bake for approximately 35-40 minutes or until a toothpick inserted into the center of the cake comes out clean.

3. **Cool and Serve**:

   - Allow the cake to cool in the pan for about 10 minutes before transferring it to a wire rack to cool completely.
   - Once cooled, dust the top lightly with powdered sugar or drizzle with a simple glaze made from lemon juice and powdered sugar for added sweetness and lemon flavor.

Flavor Profile

Sardinian Ricotta and Lemon Cake offers a wonderfully balanced taste. The ricotta provides a rich, creamy base that is perfectly complemented by the bright, citrusy notes of lemon. The cake is sweet, but not overwhelmingly so, making it an ideal dessert for those who appreciate subtlety in sweets.

Serving Suggestions

This cake is perfect as an after-dinner dessert, paired with a cup of espresso or a sweet dessert wine like Limoncello or Moscato. It can also be enjoyed as a delightful snack during the day. The lightness of the cake makes it suitable for various occasions, from family gatherings to more formal events.

Sardinian Ricotta and Lemon Cake not only brings joy to those who taste it but also honors the simple, natural ingredients that are hallmarks of Sardinian cuisine, reflecting the island's pastoral and agricultural heritage in every bite.

These recipes not only showcase the delightful flavors of Sardinia and Ikaria but also incorporate ingredients and cooking methods that contribute to the longevity of their populations.

Chapter 9:

Lifestyle Tips for Longevity: Beyond Diet

While diet plays a crucial role in the long lives of those in the Mediterranean Blue Zones, it is the integration of other lifestyle practices that completes the picture of health and longevity. This chapter explores the vital non-dietary components that contribute to a well-rounded and fulfilling life. From the importance of maintaining strong social connections and the value of daily physical activity to the practice of stress reduction and mindfulness, each aspect is deeply interwoven into the fabric of Mediterranean life. These lifestyle tips provide actionable advice on how to incorporate these age-old practices into modern living, offering readers a holistic approach to wellness that goes far beyond what's on the plate. Discover how the simple act of enjoying meals with family, embracing an active lifestyle, and finding peace in everyday moments can significantly enhance your health and extend your lifespan.

9.1 Enjoying Meals with Family and Friends: The Importance of Social Connections

In the picturesque landscapes of the Mediterranean Blue Zones, meals are more than just daily routines; they are vital social events that weave the fabric of community and family tighter with every dish served. This section dives into the pivotal role that shared meals play in enhancing life quality and promoting longevity, underscoring the profound impact of social connections developed around the dining table.

The Impact of Social Dining

Shared meals are a cornerstone of life in the Mediterranean, acting as a daily touchstone for individuals of all ages. These gatherings are not only about eating but also about exchanging stories, celebrating successes, and supporting each other during challenges. This communal approach to dining fosters a deep sense of belonging and security, contributing to lower levels of stress and higher levels of life satisfaction.

Psychological Benefits

Eating with others provides significant psychological benefits. It enhances mood, improves mental health, and reduces feelings of loneliness and isolation. In regions like Ikaria and Sardinia, where it's common for multiple generations to dine together, meals offer a chance for learning, mentorship, and the passing of traditions, enriching the social fabric of the community.

Longevity and Health

Studies have shown that strong social ties, such as those forged and sustained over shared meals, can increase longevity. These relationships help individuals cope with stress and provide a network of support that can deter unhealthy habits and encourage healthier lifestyle choices. The act of eating together also tends to slow down the pace of meals, leading to more mindful eating practices, better digestion, and improved metabolic health.

Cultural and Social Significance

In the Mediterranean, meals are often seen as celebrations, where the simple act of eating is elevated to an act of communal joy. This cultural significance of meals promotes a positive relationship with food, which is viewed not as mere sustenance but as a source of pleasure and community well-being.

Summary

The ritual of sharing meals in the Mediterranean Blue Zones is a powerful testament to the role of social connections in enhancing life quality and longevity. By prioritizing communal eating, these cultures harness the therapeutic power of companionship, turning every meal into an opportunity for nurturing the body and soul. Through this lens, we can see how integral these social practices are to the health and longevity of these communities, offering valuable lessons on the importance of nurturing relationships through the simple act of dining together.

9.2 Physical Activity in the Blue Zones: Embracing an Active Lifestyle

In the Blue Zones, where some of the world's longest-living populations reside, physical activity is not confined to gyms or exercise routines. Instead, it is seamlessly integrated into daily life through simple activities that contribute significantly to health and longevity. This section explores how these natural movements, ingrained in the everyday practices of Mediterranean societies, foster enduring health and vitality.

Natural Movement

In regions like Sardinia and Ikaria, physical activity is a natural part of the day, not a scheduled task. People frequently engage in walking to local markets, tending to gardens, or hiking through the hilly terrain. These activities are less about intentional exercise and more about living in a way that keeps the body moving regularly. The natural terrain of these areas encourages walking, which strengthens the cardiovascular system and helps maintain muscle health without the need for structured workouts.

Daily Routines

Daily chores such as cooking, cleaning, and farming also play a crucial role in keeping the residents of Blue Zones active. These tasks might not seem strenuous but require a range of movements that keep the body agile and well-conditioned. For example, kneading dough, harvesting crops, or climbing stairs to hang laundry are all physically engaging activities that burn calories, enhance coordination, and build physical resilience.

Sustainable Practices

The sustainability of these activities is key. Because they are integrated into daily life, they do not require extra motivation or the commitment of going to a gym. This integration ensures that individuals remain active throughout their lifespan, not just during their younger years. The continual engagement in physical activity contributes to a lower prevalence of obesity, hypertension, and metabolic diseases in these populations.

Longevity Benefits

Regular physical activity, as practiced in the Blue Zones, has profound benefits for longevity. It enhances cardiovascular health, reduces the risk of chronic diseases, supports mental health by reducing anxiety and depression, and helps maintain cognitive function as people age. The moderate, consistent physical engagement also helps regulate weight and metabolic processes, which are crucial for long-term health.

Social and Cultural Integration

Moreover, many of these activities are social in nature, such as participating in community dances or walking with friends. This social aspect not only makes physical activity more enjoyable but also reinforces social bonds, which are another critical component of longevity in Blue Zones.

Summary

The lesson from the Blue Zones is clear: integrating physical activity into daily life through simple, natural actions is a more sustainable and effective approach to maintaining health and extending life expectancy than sporadic, high-intensity workouts. This approach to physical activity is less about exertion and more about living in a way that keeps you moving naturally—promoting a longer, healthier life seamlessly integrated with one's environment and community.

9.3 Stress Reduction and Mindfulness: Cultivating Inner Peace

In the serene landscapes of the Mediterranean Blue Zones, the practice of reducing stress and cultivating mindfulness is not just a technique but a way of life. This section delves into how the inhabitants of regions like Sardinia and Ikaria utilize age-old practices to achieve mental and emotional balance, thereby enhancing their longevity and quality of life.

The Role of Nature

The natural settings of these regions play a crucial role in stress reduction. Residents often spend significant time outdoors, where the natural beauty and tranquility of the environment contribute to a calm mind and a relaxed body. Activities like walking through olive groves, tending to vineyards, or simply sitting by the sea allow individuals to connect with nature, which is inherently soothing and has been shown to lower cortisol levels, the body's stress hormone.

Daily Rhythms and Routines

In these communities, daily life follows a rhythmic pace that inherently discourages the rush and stress typical of modern lifestyles. This includes siestas in the afternoon, slow-paced meals, and a general cultural disdain for the hurried life. Such routines encourage living in the present moment and appreciating life's simple pleasures—key tenets of mindfulness.

Community and Social Support

The strong social support networks characteristic of Blue Zones also play a vital role in stress reduction. Regular social interactions, whether through community gatherings, group meals, or religious services, provide emotional support and a sense of belonging. Knowing that one is part of a community can significantly alleviate feelings of anxiety and depression.

Mindfulness Practices

Mindfulness, the practice of being present and fully engaged with whatever you're doing, without distraction or judgment, is naturally embedded in their daily activities. Whether it's through cooking, gardening, or crafting, these acts become meditative and reflective, not merely chores or hobbies. This mindfulness extends to eating habits as well, where meals are eaten slowly and with intention, allowing for enjoyment and proper digestion.

Breathing and Meditation

Breathing techniques and meditation are also integral to these cultures, though they may not always be formal practices. For example, spending time in quiet reflection at the end of the day, or participating in religious and spiritual activities, can serve as powerful meditative practices. These activities help in grounding the individual, fostering a peaceful state of mind, and improving overall mental health.

The Role of Arts and Culture

Engagement with the arts, whether through music, dance, or painting, is another form of mindfulness practice prevalent in these regions. These cultural activities offer expressive outlets that help reduce stress and promote happiness and satisfaction.

Summary

In conclusion, the techniques for achieving mental and emotional balance in the Blue Zones are deeply woven into the fabric of daily life. From the calming influence of natural settings and mindful daily routines to the robust community life and cultural practices, the residents of these regions show that true mindfulness is more than just an occasional practice—it is a lifestyle that nurtures inner peace and contributes profoundly to longevity and well-being.

Conclusion:

Embracing the Mediterranean Blue Zones Diet for Health and Longevity

As we conclude our exploration of the Mediterranean Blue Zones Diet, we have traversed the sun-drenched landscapes of Sardinia and the tranquil shores of Ikaria, uncovering the secrets to their celebrated longevity and vitality. This journey has not only introduced us to the delicious flavors and traditional recipes of these regions but has also illuminated the comprehensive lifestyle practices that support health and enhance lifespan.

Key Takeaways

1. **Whole Foods and Plant-Based Diet**: At the core of the Mediterranean Blue Zones diet is the emphasis on whole, plant-based foods. Fresh vegetables, fruits, legumes, whole grains, and healthy fats such as olive oil are staples that nourish the body and mind. Integrating these foods into your daily diet can significantly reduce the risk of chronic diseases and support overall well-being.

2. **Moderation and Variety**: The diet showcases a balance of flavors and nutrients, achieved through moderation and variety. It's not about restricting food groups but about enjoying them in the right amounts. This approach ensures a rich intake of different nutrients vital for the body's functions.

3. **Physical Activity as a Lifestyle**: Physical activity in the Blue Zones is naturally integrated into daily life through walking, gardening, and other physical chores. It's less about structured exercise routines and more about moving frequently at a moderate pace, which is sustainable and beneficial long-term.

4. **Community and Social Engagement**: Social connections are as nourishing as a good diet. Meals are often enjoyed in the company of family and friends, providing psychological benefits and strengthening the ties that enhance the community's health and each individual's longevity.

5. **Stress Reduction and Mindfulness**: Living in the Blue Zones involves regular practices that reduce stress and encourage mindfulness. Whether it's through quiet siestas, community interactions, or the simple act of preparing food, mindfulness permeates their way of life,

contributing to mental health and emotional balance.

Encouragement to You

As you turn the pages of this book back into your own lives, I encourage you to not just admire these practices but to integrate them into your daily routines. Start small—perhaps by incorporating more vegetables into your meals, taking daily walks, or setting aside time to connect with loved ones. Each step, no matter how small, is a step towards a healthier, fuller life.

The Journey Ahead

Embracing the *Mediterranean Blue Zones* diet and lifestyle is not merely about eating certain foods or performing specific activities; it is about cultivating a philosophy of life that values longevity through joy, community, and balance. Let the ways of life and practices you've learned here inspire you to forge a path that leads to your own health and happiness, mirroring the vibrant lives of those in Sardinia, Ikaria, and beyond.

As we conclude, remember that the journey to wellness is continuous and ever-evolving. Each choice, each meal, and each day is an opportunity to live better, not just longer. Embrace these habits with enthusiasm and see how they transform not only your health but also your entire outlook on life.

Glossary of Mediterranean Ingredients and Terms

This glossary provides a concise explanation of some of the key ingredients and terms used throughout this book, which are integral to understanding the Mediterranean Blue Zones Diet. Each entry not only defines the ingredient or concept but also briefly discusses its significance in the diet and lifestyle of the regions discussed.

Artichokes: A perennial thistle originating from the Mediterranean region, known for its edible flower buds that are rich in fiber, vitamins, and minerals.

Bottarga: Salted, cured fish roe, typically from grey mullet or bluefin tuna, often grated or sliced over pasta dishes for added flavor in Sardinian cuisine.

Cannellini Beans: White kidney beans that are a staple in Italian cooking, particularly in soups and salads. They are high in protein and fiber, contributing to heart health and digestive wellness.

Capers: Small edible flower buds, preserved in vinegar or brine, used widely in Mediterranean dishes for their tangy lemony flavor.

Fava Beans: Also known as broad beans, these legumes are a common ingredient in Mediterranean cooking, appreciated for their high protein and fiber content.

Fennel: A hardy, perennial herb with yellow flowers and a bulb used as a vegetable. Both the bulb and the seeds of the fennel plant are used in Mediterranean cuisine for their anise-like flavor.

Halloumi: A semi-hard, unripened, brined cheese made from a mixture of goat's and sheep's milk, and sometimes also cow's milk. It has a high melting point and so can easily be fried or grilled.

Ikarian: Pertaining to Ikaria, a Greek island noted for the longevity of its inhabitants, often attributed to their lifestyle and dietary habits.

Kalamata Olives: A variety of olives named after the city of Kalamata in Greece, known for their dark purple color and meaty texture.

Legumes: A class of vegetables that includes beans, lentils, and peas, known for their ability to fix nitrogen and their high fiber and protein content.

Myrtle: An evergreen shrub with aromatic, pointed leaves and star-shaped flowers, used in Sardinian cooking for flavoring roasted meats and other dishes.

Oregano: A herb from the mint family, widely used in Mediterranean cooking, known for its pungent, aromatic flavor.

Pecorino Cheese: A hard cheese made from sheep's milk, originating from Italy, known for its salty flavor and granular texture.

Phyllo Pastry: Very thin unleavened dough used for making pastries in Middle Eastern and Balkan cuisine, often used in dishes like spanakopita and baklava.

Sardinian: Pertaining to Sardinia, an Italian island renowned for its distinct and robust culinary tradition, which contributes to the longevity of its people.

Za'atar: A Middle Eastern spice mixture containing dried herbs, sesame seeds, dried sumac, and often salt, used on meats, vegetables, and baked goods.

This glossary aims to enrich your understanding of the Mediterranean Blue Zones Diet by clarifying the key elements that are essential to recreating and enjoying the recipes and meals that epitomize this healthful lifestyle.

30-Day Mediterranean Blue Zones Diet Meal Plan

Here's a 30-Day Mediterranean Blue Zones Diet Meal Plan featuring Sardinia, Italy-, and Ikaria, Greece-inspired recipes:

Day 1
Longevity Breakfast: Greek Yogurt Parfait with Honey and Walnuts
Mediterranean Lunch: Greek Salad with Feta Cheese and Kalamata Olives
Flavorful Dinner: Grilled Fish with Lemon and Garlic from Ikaria
Snack and Sweet: Ikarian Hummus with Roasted Red Pepper and Chickpeas

Day 2
Longevity Breakfast: Sardinian Frittata with Fresh Herbs and Tomatoes
Mediterranean Lunch: Sardinian Minestrone Soup with Cannellini Beans and Kale
Flavorful Dinner: Sardinian Seafood Pasta with Cherry Tomatoes and Basil
Snack and Sweet: Sardinian Olive Oil Cake with Orange Zest and Almonds

Day 3
Longevity Breakfast: Ikarian Oatmeal with Dates and Almonds

Mediterranean Lunch: Ikarian Lentil Stew with Vegetables and Herbs
Flavorful Dinner: Greek Moussaka with Eggplant and Bechamel Sauce
Snack and Sweet: Greek Baklava with Honey and Pistachios

Day 4
Longevity Breakfast: Sardinian Pane Carasau with Ricotta and Honey
Mediterranean Lunch: Sardinian Pecorino and Fig Salad
Flavorful Dinner: Sardinian Roasted Pork with Myrtle
Snack and Sweet: Sardinian Pistachio Biscotti

Day 5
Longevity Breakfast: Ikarian Herbal Tea and Fig Bars
Mediterranean Lunch: Ikarian Fisherman's Soup
Flavorful Dinner: Ikarian Longevity Stew
Snack and Sweet: Ikarian Fig and Walnut Tart

Day 6
Longevity Breakfast: Sardinian Pecorino and Pear Omelette
Mediterranean Lunch: Sardinian Pasta with Bottarga
Flavorful Dinner: Sardinian Clam and Fennel Soup
Snack and Sweet: Sardinian Honey and Almond Nougat (Torrone)

Day 7
Longevity Breakfast: Ikarian Honeyed Yogurt with Pistachios

Mediterranean Lunch: Ikarian Chickpea and Spinach Salad
Flavorful Dinner: Grilled Octopus over Ikarian Fava
Snack and Sweet: Ikarian Petimezi Cookies

Day 8
Longevity Breakfast: Sardinian Tomato and Basil Bruschetta
Mediterranean Lunch: Sardinian Roasted Lamb with Rosemary and Garlic
Flavorful Dinner: Sardinian Culurgiones
Snack and Sweet: Sardinian Seadas

Day 9
Longevity Breakfast: Ikarian Wild Green Pie (Hortopita)
Mediterranean Lunch: Ikarian Wild Herb Pie
Flavorful Dinner: Ikarian Baked Sardines
Snack and Sweet: Ikarian Herbal Tea Infusion

Day 10
Longevity Breakfast: Sardinian Artichoke and Mint Frittata
Mediterranean Lunch: Sardinian Fava Bean and Pecorino Cheese Dip
Flavorful Dinner: Sardinian Lamb with Artichokes
Snack and Sweet: Sardinian Ricotta and Lemon Cake

Day 11
Longevity Breakfast: Greek Yogurt Parfait with Honey and Walnuts
Mediterranean Lunch: Ikarian Lentil Stew with Vegetables and Herbs

Flavorful Dinner: Sardinian Roasted Pork with Myrtle
Snack and Sweet: Greek Baklava with Honey and Pistachios

Day 12
Longevity Breakfast: Sardinian Frittata with Fresh Herbs and Tomatoes
Mediterranean Lunch: Sardinian Pasta with Bottarga
Flavorful Dinner: Sardinian Seafood Pasta with Cherry Tomatoes and Basil
Snack and Sweet: Sardinian Olive Oil Cake with Orange Zest and Almonds

Day 13
Longevity Breakfast: Ikarian Oatmeal with Dates and Almonds
Mediterranean Lunch: Greek Salad with Feta Cheese and Kalamata Olives
Flavorful Dinner: Ikarian Longevity Stew
Snack and Sweet: Sardinian Honey and Almond Nougat (Torrone)

Day 14
Longevity Breakfast: Sardinian Pane Carasau with Ricotta and Honey
Mediterranean Lunch: Sardinian Minestrone Soup with Cannellini Beans and Kale
Flavorful Dinner: Grilled Octopus over Ikarian Fava
Snack and Sweet: Ikarian Petimezi Cookies

Day 15
Longevity Breakfast: Ikarian Herbal Tea and Fig Bars

Mediterranean Lunch: Ikarian Fisherman's Soup
Flavorful Dinner: Grilled Fish with Lemon and Garlic from Ikaria
Snack and Sweet: Sardinian Pistachio Biscotti

Day 16
Longevity Breakfast: Sardinian Pecorino and Pear Omelette
Mediterranean Lunch: Ikarian Chickpea and Spinach Salad
Flavorful Dinner: Ikarian Baked Sardines
Snack and Sweet: Ikarian Herbal Tea Infusion

Day 17
Longevity Breakfast: Ikarian Honeyed Yogurt with Pistachios
Mediterranean Lunch: Sardinian Roasted Lamb with Rosemary and Garlic
Flavorful Dinner: Sardinian Clam and Fennel Soup
Snack and Sweet: Ikarian Fig and Walnut Tart

Day 18
Longevity Breakfast: Sardinian Tomato and Basil Bruschetta
Mediterranean Lunch: Sardinian Fava Bean and Pecorino Cheese Dip
Flavorful Dinner: Sardinian Culurgiones
Snack and Sweet: Sardinian Seadas

Day 19
Longevity Breakfast: Ikarian Wild Green Pie (Hortopita)
Mediterranean Lunch: Sardinian Pecorino and Fig

Salad
Flavorful Dinner: Sardinian Lamb with Artichokes
Snack and Sweet: Sardinian Ricotta and Lemon Cake

Day 20
Longevity Breakfast: Greek Yogurt Parfait with Honey and Walnuts
Mediterranean Lunch: Ikarian Lentil Stew with Vegetables and Herbs
Flavorful Dinner: Grilled Fish with Lemon and Garlic from Ikaria
Snack and Sweet: Greek Baklava with Honey and Pistachios

Day 21
Longevity Breakfast: Sardinian Frittata with Fresh Herbs and Tomatoes
Mediterranean Lunch: Greek Salad with Feta Cheese and Kalamata Olives
Flavorful Dinner: Sardinian Seafood Pasta with Cherry Tomatoes and Basil
Snack and Sweet: Sardinian Olive Oil Cake with Orange Zest and Almonds

Day 22
Longevity Breakfast: Ikarian Oatmeal with Dates and Almonds
Mediterranean Lunch: Sardinian Minestrone Soup with Cannellini Beans and Kale
Flavorful Dinner: Sardinian Roasted Pork with Myrtle

Snack and Sweet: Sardinian Honey and Almond Nougat (Torrone)

Day 23

Longevity Breakfast: Sardinian Pane Carasau with Ricotta and Honey
Mediterranean Lunch: Sardinian Pasta with Bottarga
Flavorful Dinner: Ikarian Longevity Stew
Snack and Sweet: Ikarian Petimezi Cookies

Day 24

Longevity Breakfast: Ikarian Herbal Tea and Fig Bars
Mediterranean Lunch: Ikarian Fisherman's Soup
Flavorful Dinner: Grilled Octopus over Ikarian Fava
Snack and Sweet: Sardinian Pistachio Biscotti

Day 25

Longevity Breakfast: Sardinian Pecorino and Pear Omelette
Mediterranean Lunch: Ikarian Chickpea and Spinach Salad
Flavorful Dinner: Ikarian Baked Sardines
Snack and Sweet: Ikarian Herbal Tea Infusion

Day 26

Longevity Breakfast: Ikarian Honeyed Yogurt with Pistachios
Mediterranean Lunch: Sardinian Roasted Lamb with Rosemary and Garlic
Flavorful Dinner: Sardinian Clam and Fennel Soup
Snack and Sweet: Ikarian Fig and Walnut Tart

Day 27

Longevity Breakfast: Sardinian Tomato and Basil Bruschetta

Mediterranean Lunch: Sardinian Fava Bean and Pecorino Cheese Dip

Flavorful Dinner: Sardinian Culurgiones

Snack and Sweet: Sardinian Seadas

Day 28

Longevity Breakfast: Ikarian Wild Green Pie (Hortopita)

Mediterranean Lunch: Sardinian Pecorino and Fig Salad

Flavorful Dinner: Sardinian Lamb with Artichokes

Snack and Sweet: Sardinian Ricotta and Lemon Cake

Day 29

Longevity Breakfast: Sardinian Artichoke and Mint Frittata

Mediterranean Lunch: Greek Salad with Feta Cheese and Kalamata Olives

Flavorful Dinner: Grilled Fish with Lemon and Garlic from Ikaria

Snack and Sweet: Greek Baklava with Honey and Pistachios

Day 30

Longevity Breakfast: Greek Yogurt Parfait with Honey and Walnuts

Mediterranean Lunch: Ikarian Lentil Stew with Vegetables and Herbs

Flavorful Dinner: Sardinian Seafood Pasta with Cherry

Tomatoes and Basil
Snack and Sweet: Sardinian Olive Oil Cake with Orange Zest and Almonds

This meal plan rotates through a variety of healthful and flavorful recipes inspired by the Mediterranean Blue Zones of Sardinia and Ikaria, aiming to bring the benefits of their longevity diets into your everyday life.

Acknowledgments

In crafting this journey through the Mediterranean Blue Zones, I am indebted to a chorus of invaluable voices and sources. From the local chefs and families in Sardinia and Ikaria who generously shared their culinary secrets and personal stories, to the researchers and experts whose studies into longevity have illuminated the path to healthier living, this book stands as a testament to their collective wisdom.

Special thanks are due to the culinary historians and nutritionists who provided critical insights that shaped the narrative of traditional diets and their impact on long life and wellness. Their meticulous work has helped bridge the gap between ancient practices and contemporary understanding.

I must also acknowledge the countless hours spent by my editorial team, whose expertise and dedication ensured that the cultural nuances and nutritional information were presented accurately and engagingly. Their commitment to excellence has been essential in bringing this project to fruition.

To my family and friends, who endured numerous recipe tests and tasted endless iterations of meals, your patience and feedback were vital in refining this collection to ensure authenticity and enjoyment.

Lastly, I extend my gratitude to you, the reader, for embarking on this journey to discover the Mediterranean Blue Zones. Your commitment to exploring new ways to enrich your health and extend your life is inspiring. Together, through these pages, we embrace the time-honored traditions that promise not just years to our life, but life to our years.